Secrets of a Successful Jewelry Brand:

How to Take Your Home Jewelry Business to the Next Level

By Efy Tal with Noa Tal

Secrets of a Successful Jewelry Brand
How to Take Your Home Business to the Next Level

Published by Pandora Press:
© Pandora Press 2014 All rights reserved.
ISBN: 978-0-9914532-1-4

Terms and Conditions:
The purchaser of this book is subject to the condition that he/she shall in no way resell it, nor any part of it, nor make copies of it to distribute freely. No part of this book may be used or reproduced in any manner whatsoever without written permission except in the case of brief quotations embodied in critical articles and reviews.

Table of Contents

Chapter 1 - What this Book Offers 6
   What I Will (and Won't) Discuss 7
   About Me and How Became A Success 10
   Why Am I Writing this Book? 11
Chapter 2 - Getting Started on Your Business 13
   How Much Money Do You Need? 14
   Miscellaneous Items 17
   A Day in the Life 19
Chapter 3 - Product Development and Design Tips 23
   Finding Your Own Look 24
   Artistry vs. Profit 27
   Creating Your Own Castings 30
   Precious Metal Clay 30
   Wax Models 32
   Computer-Aided Design 33
   Factory Casting 33
   Labor-Intensive vs. Simple Assembly 34
   Made in the USA vs. Outsourcing 36
   High Material Cost vs. Low Material Cost 37
   Pricing Individually and in Bulk 40
   Pieces per Line 41
   Frequency of New Product Development 43
   Case Study: Dogeared 44
Chapter 4 - Creating Samples 46
   Samples Explained 47
   Sample Boards 47
   Sample Selection and Editing 54
   Line Sheets 55
Chapter 5 - Branding and Marketing 58
   Designing a Logo 60
   Taking Professional Pictures 61
   Tags (Metal and Cardboard) and Earring Cards 64
   Developing Your Story 69
   Shelf Talkers and Brand Markers 71
   Look-Book 73

- Website 75
- Social Media 79
- Press 81
- Chapter 6 - Production 86
  - Manufacturing 87
  - In the U.S. 89
  - Overseas 91
  - Assembly 94
- Chapter 7-How to Automate Your Business Through Employees 98
  - Making your Jewelry 100
  - Other Ways to Automate 104
- Chapter 8 - Getting Your Line into Stores on Your Own 106
  - Types of Stores to Target 107
  - How to Approach Stores 114
  - Territories 117
  - Conflicts of Interest 118
- Chapter 9 - "Reps" 120
  - What You Should Expect from Your Rep 121
  - Finding Reps 124
  - What to Do When you Find a Rep 128
  - Things to Discuss When Interviewing a Rep 130
- Chapter 10 - What to Expect at Tradeshows 132
  - What is a Tradeshow? 133
  - Having Your Own Booth 135
  - Being Represented by a Rep at a Tradeshow 140
  - Showrooms 144
- Chapter 11 - Account Management 146
  - Receiving Orders 147
  - Processing and Shipping Orders 149
  - Client Relations 153
- Chapter 12 - Selling Discontinued and Overstock Items 155
  - Craft Fairs and Farmers Markets 156
  - Sample Sales 157
  - Consignment Stores 158
  - Give-Aways! 158
  - Off-Price Retailers 159
  - Deal Websites 159
  - Jewelry Parties and Trunk Shows 159
  - Your Own Online Shops 160

Table of Contents

Chapter 1

What this Book Offers

What this Book Offers

What I Will (and Won't*) Discuss*

This is not a book on how to make jewelry. I'm not going to show you how to start selling it through at-home parties, trunk shows, or local craft markets. I have done all of the above and certainly have a lot to say, but there are already plenty of books discussing these subjects. What I am here to do is something almost none of the others have: discuss how to bring your jewelry business to the next level. I want to show you how to actually *live* off of your jewelry business, creating a viable brand carried in hundreds of stores across the country. This is not a book about hobbies, but turning a beloved pastime into a bustling, sustainable, jewelry-specific business.

If you are reading this book, I assume you already know how to make jewelry, have a general aesthetic sense, and believe that people like your jewelry (and might be willing to pay money for it)! Perhaps you're already selling to friends and family, or even a larger circle. Perhaps you have started selling online. Regardless of whether you've started sales or have never made a piece for profit, I've filled each page with facts, hints, and anecdotes to help you hone your skills.

The number one question I get asked by aspiring designers is "where do you get all these road reps to sell your line for you?" I'm also often asked about tradeshows: Did you know that so much business takes place and connections are established at gift and accessories tradeshows? Which tradeshows? What goes on in these tradeshows? How much does it cost to participate? What do you need to exhibit and do well? Another important question: "Should I exhibit my line in a showroom?" "How do I begin to find someone to manufacture my designs for me?" Before writing this book I wanted to know if there are any resources out there answering these questions and I have not found a single source or book explaining how to go about finding these reps, how to succeed at tradeshows, how to get designs manufactured, how to create professional looking samples, what to do with overstock, and so on. I'm going to teach you all these things in this book.

I will also teach you to automate your jewelry business so that it can run without your daily involvement. Like other businesses, this is one where you can create a stand-alone company, where you work "on" your business rather than "in" your business, making you a creative head and not a slave to daily chores. To that aim, this book will help you develop the business skills crucial to running a jewelry business, which I will demonstrate are just as important, if not more so, than jewelry-making skills themselves. In writing this book, I want to help you develop your business acumen, people management skills, creativity, and dedication to your craft. You will also acquire a new perspective on how to view your business and your role in it. All in all, you will learn specific information, details, and great tips on the ins and outs of getting to the next level.

Another broad topic I will not address in this book is the more technical, legal side of opening a business. (There are heaps of books already in print on this at your local library, bookstore, or online shop.) This includes issues such as incorporation (what type of entity, where and how to incorporate), tax considerations, legal ramifications of hiring employees, payroll issues, and the like. While this sort of information can be helpful, even essential, to stating your business, we are more concerned with the opening and running of a jewelry business. General business and legal topics mainly fall outside this book's scope and are not addressed.

Typically, this book will appeal to those with the intention of creating a jewelry business that they can live on or with the desire to create a side business where they can express creativity and make a buck doing something fun. Whether you achieve the former or the latter really depends on your personal goals and the amount of time and money that you choose to invest in your business. (For the sake of illustration, if your goal is to live off the wholesale portion of your business alone, you should be targeting at least one wholesale order per day at an average order price of $500.) By the time you finish reading, you will have the knowledge necessary to build a successful jewelry business from the ground-up!

About Me and How Became A Success

You might ask– what makes me qualified to write a book like this? Currently, I own the successful mid-market line Efy Tal Jewelry that is carried in over 200 stores all over the United States.

Honestly, I've been a jewelry-holic all my life. I started taking jewelry classes in high school and college and loved every moment of it. However, I chose a career in engineering during college and worked as an engineer for thirteen years. But, my love affair with jewelry didn't stop there. In 2002, I started making jewelry and selling it at local craft markets. I was doing extremely well with sales but ran into a problem: the more I sold, the harder I had to work to keep up with the sales, because I made every single item that I sold, and each piece was uniquely designed and hand-crafted by me.

A few years in, my world was turned upside down when all of my jewelry and equipment was stolen during a move. I stopped designing for a few years, overwhelmed at the thought of starting over from scratch and having to replenish my stock, equipment, and designs from zero. With the encouragement of my husband, I started designing again in 2007, but with a completely new frame of mind. That time, I started redeveloping the business with a new focus on efficiency and practicality, knowing that I wanted to set things up in a way that I would not end up a slave to the business again.

With renewed vigor, I managed to get the business up and running to the point where I would have been able to fully support myself financially off of local market sales and wholesale locations. However, I still had my engineering job (yes, it was a very busy time), so my focus was split between my day-job and my passion project.

In 2011, my husband and I moved from California to New York. I took a leap of faith and quit my engineering job to focus on jewelry full-time, take the business to the next level, and raise our daughter Lia. I have now been devoted to the jewelry business full-time for two years and it has grown in ways I never previously imagined. I am proud to say that I can more than comfortably support myself financially from this business alone. I have also shifted much of my focus to online sales, which now represent a significant revenue stream, in addition to sales from physical store locations.

Why Am I Writing this Book?

Now, why would someone with a successful business take the time to write a book, as opposed to focusing purely on that business? As mentioned before, the goal of a truly successful business is to focus "on" the business, as opposed to working "in" the business. What I mean is that, though I do focus on business-related activities full-time, I am now in a position where, rather than dealing with manufacturing and assembling jewelry, plus processing daily orders, I am able to focus on growing the business strategically. This includes finding new venues for my jewelry, adding new revenue streams, as well as offering new types of products to my customers, such as informational products. With this book, I hope to create synergy and complementarity with my line and ultimately continue grow my business to new levels. With any luck, you find the information in this book as priceless as it is to me. In all of my research when I was starting out, I could not find a comprehensive informational resource for bringing an at-home jewelry business to the point where it is sold nationally and, most importantly, on income a designer can live on. I just knew a book like this would have saved me a lot of time and heartache, and I am therefore confident that it will do so for you! Let's get going!

Chapter 2

Getting Started on Your Business

How Much Money Do You Need?

It is always important to think about the simple nuts and bolts of starting your business, so this chapter will discuss basic set-up information, as well as what you should expect to be busy with on a daily basis once you're up and running. Let's get started with finances.

The good news is that starting a jewelry business does not have to be too capital-intensive, at least at the beginning, if your goals are not too ambitious. I actually started my business with about $1,000. With that money, I purchased actual jewelry components, such as chain and stones and small tools. When I started, I was focusing on selling jewelry in local markets rather than stores, so some of my start-up money went towards display materials. The $1,000 is an absolute minimum, in the case of mid-level jewelry using silver or gold-plate and semi-precious stones anyway, assuming you have small initial expectations and a clear vision of your line.

In my case, I was able to grow the business organically, reinvesting profits without really putting in additional out-of-pocket funds or seeking outside investment. I accomplished this because, for a long time, everything I made from the business went right back into it, enabling it to grow. This method of profit reinvestment has the benefit of being self-containing and fiscally responsible, but it delays being able to take money out of the business for personal use. Plus, your growth will be slow and it will be necessary to have another source of income meanwhile.

Investing capital along with what one makes in profits will allow a business to grow more quickly than just reinvesting the profits alone. It is clear to me now that I could have grown my business much more quickly if I had invested capital in addition to what I was generating from sales. For example, I did not hire employees right away, which I could have done with some invested capital. What I have realized in hindsight is making all of the jewelry myself diverted my attention from more productive activities, like coming up with additional sale venues. Drawing from my experiences, I'd recommend setting aside a budget for hiring at least one part-time helper when you launch your business. Roughly speaking, I would suggest that you set aside an additional $1,000 for your first month of employee help if you plan to hire someone right away. I will talk more about employees in Chapter 7, "Automating Your Business Through Employees".

I also did not have a professional website when I started. A website does not necessarily need to be designed by a professional but, depending on your skill level, making a website that looks well put together with professional pictures may cost you some money. Taking beautiful photographs of your jewelry is critically important and, unless you are a professional photographer, your chances of coming up with anything remotely polished enough to compete with other jewelry on the web are slim to none. In my own case, my husband and I spent months trying all kinds of different backgrounds, lighting, and camera equipment in an attempt to achieve professional-looking pictures ourselves. We ended up using *none* of them. So, I highly recommend you set aside about $2,000 for pictures, which will be worth your while and save you precious time.

All in all, assuming that you buy enough materials for your first round of samples (not counting inventory, which you can purchase later with money from sales or with additional capital), that you hire at least one part-time helper, and that you get professional pictures taken, we're totaling $4,000. However, given that you may want to invest in *some* inventory right off the bat, which will be expensive, or that there may be other incidental costs, you should really budget a total of about $6,000 before you embark on your business journey. This will allow you to begin operations on a lean, but viable, budget.

One additional consideration when it comes to money is that, although you can technically start your business with the $6,000 with minimal inventory, it is difficult to predict what your customers will order and how much inventory you will need to keep in stock. Admittedly, it takes time to get the hang of this as you get the feel for your business. If you choose to start small and re-stock inventory in small amounts as you need it to fill sales orders, you should know that you will not be getting the preferential pricing terms that jewelry makers with larger orders will get. You can invest more in inventory and get better pricing on bigger orders, or you can start lean and know that, while you are growing, individual components will cost you more. Ultimately, the better route is to try and obtain preferential pricing off the bat, but this choice might be dictated by your financial situation. You'll have to choose what works best for you.

Miscellaneous Items

In addition to finding space, materials, and equipment necessary for your particular type of jewelry designs, you will want to invest in a few additional business tools right away: a fax/copy/scan machine for receiving orders and making copies, a computer (of course), potentially a kiln, and the ability to process credit card payments. Although you might assume that you can run some of your business orders and payments via the internet and that faxes are so last millennium, you should know that most physical stores and representatives that you will hire to sell your jewelry to stores, or 'reps', aren't as technologically savvy, and won't make orders online. Most reps fax orders and will be unwilling to change their normal business practice for your sake if you do not have a fax machine. While you can obtain a fax number that will send the fax to your email, the copy and scan parts of the machine will be used on a regular basis.

Secrets of a Successful Jewelry Brand

The vast majority of my store accounts and individual customers pay via credit card. When a customer is ready to make a payment, it is essential that you be ready to process that payment right away from day one. You will therefore need the enable credit card processing ASAP. These quirks may seem counter-intuitive in this modern technological age but, as of today you will need these tools to succeed in the jewelry business. I use Merchant Warehouse as my credit card processor; it has the lowest fees I could find.

My Studio

Getting Started on Your Business

My Beautiful Wall of Components and Stones

A Day in the Life

You may be wondering at this point, once you get your business up and running, what does a jewelry designer do on a daily basis at his or her studio? I have put together a list of a number of tasks that I do regularly, which are either things that only I can do or that I might be training someone else to do eventually, but that I like to have my eye on. Since the goal of a business owner is to work "on" their business rather than "in" their business, I am constantly searching for ways to automate more and more tasks and to train my employees to take on additional challenges.

The following list consists of items that, as of right now, I actually spend my day-to-day doing myself, which includes mainly creative or business-generating activities. Also, I try to personally invest time only on tasks that will generate a long-term benefit for my business, as opposed to daily tasks that I can hand down to my employees. Here is a list of tasks that I handle personally as of today:

- Designing new jewelry styles
- Training and empowering my employees
- Searching for new customers, reps, and suppliers
- Bookkeeping/accounting and paying bills
- Working on marketing, logos and branding
- Optimizing my website (Google analytics, content, etc.)
- Developing new growth strategies for my brand, such as writing this book
- Networking with other business owners
- Email marketing campaigns
- Video marketing
- Business courses (all online)
- Studying more successful brands to gain insight into what they are doing and generate new ideas
- Developing relationship with existing customers, reps, and suppliers
- Managing social media, such as Facebook and blog content

- Working on automation systems for the business (how to find inventory and style numbers quickly or new organizational techniques)
- Other creative tasks such as creating new revenue streams

This list is just an idea of what tasks you should ideally be focused on once you bring your business "to the next level", though you may not be there yet. I will go on to discuss many aspects of these activities, as well as how to empower your employees to take on various day-to-day tasks that can be automated, so as to free you up for the more creative and long-term growth-oriented work. I work about 3-4 hours a day because I take care of my daughter and I don't want to be a full time employee in my business. But, if I had more time to spend at this stage of my business, I would concentrate on building my network, my audience, and my reach through growing my mailing list, writing more/better blog posts, engaging in more social media, expanding my email marketing campaigns, developing my partnerships with people in the business, and working on my relationships with reps and stores. I would also continue to oversee the improvement and optimization of my websites, and continue to open new online revenue streams, as well as continue to study my competition and other businesses that inspire me.

Chapter 3

Product Development and Design Tips

Product Development and Design Tips

Finding Your Own Look

When a customer picks up a piece of jewelry from your collection, there should be something that immediately lets the customer know that the piece is one of yours. This is what we in the jewelry industry call cultivating a "signature look". A signature look does not have to be something that is duplicated in its entirety from piece to piece, but rather a certain inspiration that can be traced back to your brand. You will want to consider carefully what your inspiration is and try and make sure, to the extent possible, that most of the pieces in your collection somehow fit your theme. Of course, there will be times where, you may have to sacrifice some of the more costly elements of your designs in favor of less expensive or more high-selling solutions, but, for the most part, it is very difficult to become a successful jewelry *brand* without some kind of signature look. There are many things to weigh when coming up with a signature look. What your signature look will be is entirely up to you and your imagination. But, you should consider that while, on the one hand, a signature look must be unique, it should appeal to a broad base of customers. Being too niche could limit your potential market reach. If you happen to have a very eccentric or out-of-the box type of look, which is great in terms of individuality and potential for identification, consider drawing from pure inspiration and distilling it a bit to create a look that is both identifiable as you and at the same time somewhat commercial.

While great examples of jewelry design is everywhere, some of my favorite designers with unmistakable yet marketable unique looks are Anna Beck with her gold dots over silver geometric shapes, Ayala Bar and her colorful Byzantine beaded mosaics and faceted glass, and Lois Hill with her intricate Indonesian silver dots and swirls. Anna Beck's designs are based on one specific idea, though you may want to think slightly less specific for starters. She is extremely successful, but it is more difficult to build a brand on such a narrow look. Ayala Bar and Lois Hill, in my opinion, strike a more approachable balance between uniqueness and commerciality by providing a wider range of designs.

My signature look is nature-inspired, both plants and animals, with rose gold detail over a silver setting with bezel-set stones.

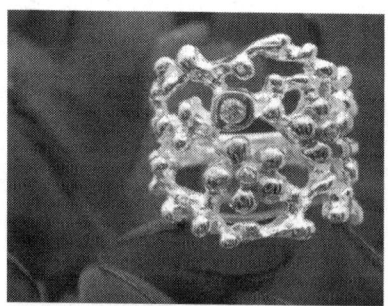

Efy Tal Jewelry Sample 1

Product Development and Design Tips

Efy Tal Jewelry Sample 2

Efy Tal Jewelry Sample 3

I also finish every piece with a signature stamped "Efy" tag accompanied by a small freshwater pearl. This, along with my unique take on design, makes my pieces identifiable as Efy Tal jewelry.

Secrets of a Successful Jewelry Brand

Artistry vs. Profit

You may be surprised that this book would address the topic of artistry with an audience of jewelry makers who are, by and large, artists. While most of us are inspired to start out of a love of artistry and craftsmanship, it is important to learn how to balance artistic and business interests if you want to make your jewelry business a success. Even if you already have established jewelry designs that are selling, you may still want to seriously consider the points raised in this section before growing your business further.

Very early in my jewelry career, when my line broke into its very first store, I was lucky enough to have a very savvy and experienced store owner as a customer. She took me under her wing and mentored me on these concepts I'm sharing with you. Back then, I was full of creativity and yet green as a leaf when it came to business. (I remember thinking, during our discussions, that the information she imparted was gold and that I would be putting it in a book one day.) The first thing that my mentor told me is that a jewelry designer has to confront a fundamental question right off the bat: you must decide if it is more important to make art or to make money. It goes without saying that both art and money are important components in a jewelry business. But ultimately, if your focus is 'art for art's sake', you will hit many a crossroad where you find yourself compromising your livelihood and the viability of your business. When confronted with this question, though I am by nature a very creative person, I knew I

Product Development and Design Tips

would have to choose money. I realized that art, creativity, and uniqueness are necessary and fulfilling elements that you must express, but only within the constraints of creating economically feasible pieces.

Here's an example from my own experience. I am currently wrapping up a bridal line, which is simple, not too original, but which I know will sell. I had an amazing time creatively designing beautiful packaging and presentation around the line and collaborating on amazing photography of the pieces. However, the jewelry itself is simple because I realized that this is a niche market where simple designs will sell.

I confess, the bridal line is not my most innovative work. But a wedding is a time where people expect to spend some money, buy things like jewelry, in MULTIPLES and it made sense to get a piece of this market. Imagine having to buy ten pieces of jewelry for an entire bridal party – it could cost a fortune! Niche lines like this can make you the money you need to fund other more creative endeavors that may not be as lucrative, or to make up for losses on designs that simply don't sell as expected. You can, and should, have a few pieces in your line that define you as a designer, but you need to fill out your line with pieces that sell, which are often not the most elaborate, and with pieces that you can manufacture cost-efficiently.

If you are not convinced yet, and your answer to the art vs. money question remains art, keep in mind what you will be facing down the road. By definition, you will be sacrificing low costs, efficiency, and your only real targets as customers will be the high-end departments of high-end stores such as Saks Fifth Avenue or Bergdorf Goodman. There may be a bit of latitude for buyers to have little to no consideration of cost because their customers, in turn, will pay astronomical amounts for jewelry. Unfortunately, the chance of getting picked up by such stores is extremely low in general, especially if you have not yet broken into regular stores.

It goes without saying that you will need to strike a balance between creativity and cost-cutting. Every designer must find his or her own voice, and it is important to find and nurture this uniqueness within you. However, you have to learn to harness that creativity to fit within the parameters allowed by practical business sense. Cutting yourself off from most of your potential customers because your costs are just too high is an easy way to fail at business fast. If you can convince yourself to work within the constraints of what is economically efficient and the balance between what your customers want and are willing to
pay for, you will be much better off, and sooner.

Creating Your Own Castings

There are many people making jewelry these days that never make their own castings. Instead, they go to gem shows and buy pre-made metal castings that are attractive and salable, but lack a unique quality. It is possible to find basically every type of casting at many fairs and online and there are many designers who

Product Development and Design Tips

draw from this never-ending pool of already-cast pieces to create beautiful jewelry. However, if you want to become a higher-level jewelry designer and be considered as such by discriminating buyers in galleries and boutiques, it will be necessary to create your own metal castings. Alternatively, if you do not use metal castings, you will still need some completely original component or technique that competitors cannot make without infringing on your designs.

If you have been trained in professional jewelry-making technique to make your own molds and have access to a professional-grade studio, then you are very likely already making your own unique designs. But, making your own unique designs does not necessarily require a highly-skilled jewelry technician or state-of-the-art space and equipment.

Precious Metal Clay

The best material I have found for creating original casting is precious metal clay. The two main brand names are PMC and Art Clay. It almost goes without saying that the easiest way to order this material is online. One authority website for using this material is www.cooltools.us and another is (of course, as the authority for anything-jewelry) www.riogrande.com. Between these two sites, you should have ample access to everything you will need to create your own designs with precious metal clay.

Most people do not think of this medium as a solution for making originals for casting. Precious metal clay is most-often used by people who just want to make one piece of jewelry for themselves. However, it is an extremely versatile substance that is actually wonderful for creating originals and will allow you make them more quickly and with less technical training than any other technique I know. In addition, it used to come only in only silver and gold, but it is also now available in bronze, copper, and other metals.

You can search your local community for classes in using this substance and, in a matter of hours, can develop the techniques needed to create great original pieces for casting. I became certified in using precious metal clay early in my career and, unless you are already a professionally-trained jeweler, I highly recommend investing some time perfecting this technique, since it will yield the highest return on your time. Becoming a pro at creating your own designs with precious metal clay is a matter of practicing for days or weeks, as opposed to the years it can take to master other professional jewelry-making techniques. A design that you make with precious metal clay will look like any other piece of metal jewelry that you can send to get cast by a manufacturers.

Other ways of creating your own designs include hiring someone to create wax models for you, hiring someone to create CAD drawings for you, or, when working with factories overseas, you can send them drawings and let them create your molds from those drawings and specs.

Wax Models

Regarding wax models, jewelers who are hired to work for someone else make very little money and often times are happy to have side jobs. One wax piece commissioned from one of these jewelers could cost anywhere between $150 and $300. But, if you want to have many pieces commissioned and can find someone to work by the hour, you may be able to get the overall price down to somewhere around $30-$40 per piece. To find a jeweler who could use extra work, you can post a jobs ad on Craigslist or go to your local jewelry exchange. You may have to try a few jewelers before you find one whose quality and reliability you are happy with, but once you find a great fit, you can work with them for a long time. I have used this wax piece method for several of my pieces and have been very happy with the results.

Computer-Aided Design

CAD (computer-aided design) drawings are another great way to make your own molds. While there is no shortage of services that you can easily find online that will produce CAD designs for you, I think the best way to do this cheaply is to find a student at either a jewelry program or an art school. This is because they are learning the most up-to-date techniques for producing these drawings and are happy to test out their new skills cheaply because they have no job experience. The best way to get in touch with students who can help with this is to find your local jewelry or art schools and put ads up for the job, or ask an administrator or faculty to recommend names.

Factory Casting

If you choose to work with a factory overseas for manufacturing, one of the services these factories can offer, included in the price of manufacturing, is to create pieces for you on the basis of drawings that you send them. A drawback here can be that you may have to produce rather detailed designs, using extremely simple English in the annotations. You may also have to be in touch with them and make corrections until the sample molds are up to your standards. Nevertheless, this process can yield satisfying results and is convenient because, if you are choosing this method for manufacturing anyway, then
this extra design help is usually included.

Labor-Intensive vs. Simple Assembly

It is important to consider how labor-intensive your pieces will be to produce. If you choose to create pieces that are extremely labor-intensive, meaning that they have many components and might be difficult to put together, you should know that it will take you much longer to train your employees to assemble your pieces and that you will have to create extremely detailed "recipes" for your employees to follow when creating

Product Development and Design Tips

pieces. (Recipes consist of the components of your jewelry and then any specific assembly instructions.) Also, you would be surprised how often small components of a piece of jewelry will go out of stock, become hard to come by, or for which you find a more desirable replacement. Thus, the more components per recipe, the more likely your jewelry recipes will be going out of date on a regular basis.

This section is not meant to discourage you from making your creations all that they can be, and you do not have to limit yourself to only extremely simple pieces. As an example, Dana Kellin and Ayala Bar have become very successful doing pieces that include, respectively, intricate wire wrapping techniques and many components. However, these designers probably employ a fleet of true artisans that stay with them for a long time because it takes time to train employees in the technique of making complicated labor-intensive jewelry. A last point that may seem like an obvious corollary is that if your pieces are more labor intensive and you have to pay people more to make them, you will, of course, have to charge more for your pieces. This can drastically reduce the number of customers who can afford or are willing to buy your pieces.

I find that is it not only difficult to train people in intricate assembly techniques, but it can be downright impossible in most cases. The vast majority of people who have applied to work on my business simply do not pick up assembly techniques on more than a very basic level. The people who are more artistic and end up having more talent in complicated assembly techniques will often recognize their talent and be able to command higher salaries. But, *c'est la vie*!

What I choose to do in order to minimize labor, but maximize the intricacy of my designs, is to create original molds that are as intricate as possible. That way, I get one piece back that has a lot of my uniqueness and detail right in it and yet can be assembled simply into an overall finished product. It often works much better to spend a bit of extra time on the original mold and not count on the intricacy of your pieces coming later, from various components. Such pieces will end up looking like a lot of work went into them, which will be the case, but you can do the work up front on the designing end and minimize back-end labor costs and the possibility of mistakes during assembly.

One last point I'd like to make is there are plenty of designers who only design pieces that have no assembly involved at all. Think rings, cuffs, bangles, pendants, post earrings, etc. These come from the factory and are immediately ready to ship. This may be good a strategy to think about when first starting out if you don't have the infrastructure for assembly, albeit somewhat limiting.

Product Development and Design Tips

Made in the USA vs. Outsourcing

Whether to make your jewelry in the USA or abroad is another important question to consider in the beginning and as you grow. There are certain galleries and stores that pride themselves on accepting only designers that conceive, manufacture, and assemble their lines 100% in the USA. You may find it interesting to appeal to these stores and feel it is worth the extra effort to be known as a brand that makes all of its jewelry in the USA. However, in my experience, there are not so many of these stores to warrant targeting and the ones that do can drop your line in a heartbeat, just like any other store, so it may not be worth your effort to manufacture locally if appealing to such stores is your only consideration.

You may have your own reasons for preferring to manufacture in the USA, and that is perfectly valid. But, you should know that it is virtually impossible to source all of your components from the USA, since the overwhelming majority of jewelry components are simply not made stateside. If you want to hire employees in the USA, or if you choose to assemble your line here, you can certainly state in your marketing materials that all of your jewelry is *assembled* in the USA.

High Material Cost vs. Low Material Cost

No matter what style of jewelry you choose, you will never be able to please everyone. There are some women who love larger pendants, statement pieces, and fabulous chandelier earrings. There are other women who love small, understated pieces. Whether you choose larger, more complicated pieces or smaller, simpler pieces, you will basically have as your customer the market of women who like that particular size and style of the jewelry.

Personally, I am not a 'less is more' type of jewelry wearer, but rather a 'more is more' gal. In my own wardrobe I tend to favor large, intricate pieces that I often layer together. However, it is clearly more affordable, both in terms of materials cost and labor cost, to produce smaller pieces. Therefore, although I started my line making larger statement pieces because that is my own personal style, I realized that, as a business woman, there is plenty of business to be done on the smaller scale. I have thus shifted the focus of my line somewhat to focus on smaller pieces, which sell very well.

Since you may be evaluating which demographic to favor, why not go after the one that will cost you less to produce? Smaller items tend to sell at lower prices and therefore make easier impulse buys when customers feel like treating themselves. Plus, they also make great gifts for people who are not looking to spend loads of money, especially if they have many gifts to buy. I find that having my original and intricate designs gives credibility and context for my small simple pieces.

A perfectly valid counter-argument to the suggestion that smaller pieces should be your route is "what if I want to sell fewer

Product Development and Design Tips

products at higher prices?" Of course, this is your prerogative. It is absolutely possible to deal in the very expensive jewelry market. It's just that the standards in that market can be much more exacting and, by the very nature of the fact that there are less customers and stores able to afford your product, you will have to work much harder to find them. The smaller and more affordable scale jewelry will get sold with more frequency and probably somewhat less effort. I had a rep that used to say, "Fast nickels are better than slow dimes". It is ultimately up to you whether or not you adopt this philosophy, but it is certainly worth considering the differences in strategy that your business will have to adopt depending on your choice.

A note regarding diamonds: I do not personally use diamonds in my line. They immediately make your cost and sales price skyrocket. Obviously, diamonds of considerable size and quality can sell for thousands, tens of thousands, and even millions of dollars. However, it is possible to find very small, low quality diamonds at about $5 a "milli-diamond", as they are called, if you buy in bulk. You can charge considerably more for jewelry pieces that have diamonds on them, even if they are milli-diamonds, simply because of the name of the stone. However, you may not want to set diamonds in silver because it can diminish the value of the diamond. Basically, using diamonds means that you will have to start dealing in gold or other more expensive precious metal along with the fact that you will need a professional jeweler to set your stones. You are therefore left more vulnerable to fluctuations in the price of gold and other precious metals in addition to the price of diamonds, which fluctuate more and with higher amplitude than less expensive and less sought-after stone varieties. It has not made sense for me to include diamonds in my business, but you should always consider if it makes sense for you.

Pricing Individually and in Bulk

Buyers who purchase wholesale jewelry generally expect to pay very little for it compared to what you might assume you could charge. There is a lot of competition in the jewelry industry and buyers usually mark-up pieces 2.5 to 3 times before selling them to the final consumer. Therefore, when pricing your pieces, you have to consider what you think an end customer will be willing to pay for a piece and basically divide that number by at least 2.5. That is the amount you will likely be able to sell to a store. You therefore have to make sure that your total costs, materials + labor + operating expenses + commission, are a fair amount below one half of the end-price of a piece if you expect to make a profit.

Also, since the beginning of the current economic recession in 2008, there has been a trend towards stores demanding even lower pricing. My reps tell me that there are many stores now that will not accept pieces unless they can retail to the final consumer at under $50. Of course, doing the math, it means I have to sell them to the store for under $20 per piece and this may not seem to leave much margin.

Product Development and Design Tips

In order to make money on the pieces, I therefore have to use a similar formula to the one that stores use to calculate whether or not a piece will be worthwhile to make. I calculate the price of making a piece and I multiply that by 3. I only make the piece if I believe I can sell it for that number. In the case of a piece that needs to be sold wholesale at $20, that means that I need to be able to make it for around $7, including everything. If $7 goes towards these direct costs, about another $7 goes to rep commissions and other costs of running the business, and about $7 is left for profit. You can probably calculate similarly in your business - about 1/3 of wholesale price for direct material and labor costs, an extra 1/3 towards other costs, and about 1/3 for profit.

Again, these margins may not seem big, but jewelry is most often a high-volume business. It is very difficult to make big money on individual pieces unless you are using extremely expensive components, such as diamonds. Remember also that the example just given is the very low end of what might be found in your average store. The average piece of jewelry does, of course, retail for well above $50, which means you can sell it to a store for well above $20, and your profit is therefore also higher that explained above.

Pieces per Line

If you started your line selling jewelry at markets or at house jewelry parties, you might have hundreds and hundreds of individual pieces you created without much thought towards creating a cohesive collection. However, if you want to be able to sell in many stores and to customers across the country, you will have to edit down the number of pieces you display and decide on a collection of items that you will feature as being available for wholesale at any given time. To have a mature, complete line, stores expect to see about 20 sample boards, which will be discussed in a later chapter. Each sample board typically contains about 5-8 pieces, making a full line somewhere around 100 individual jewelry pieces.

You will often run into designers that have 50 or 60 boards to display at any one time, but this is usually not by design and is not necessarily a good thing. It usually means that the designers are not discontinuing older styles and recalling them. Failing to edit your collection and recall old items as you create new ones will not often work in your favor, because buyers do not typically want to look at more than about 20 sample boards. You may therefore be forced to show some weaker pieces at the expense of stronger ones, if you are not able to show your whole collection. Buyers may also decide that your collection is frazzled and not cohesive if it looks cluttered and fail to buy for that reason.

I will concede that it is difficult for designers to discontinue and recall pieces because it requires reps to repackage the whole line, ship it back, and wait for you to re-do your sample boards. Reps usually have neither the time nor the inclination to do this because they work on commission. Most reps will agree to send back your line for renewing of sample boards about once a year. But, the more you can stay on top of them and attempt to keep your collection as close to the acceptable 100-or-so pieces, the better your collection will present to buyers. It is also important to stay on top of this issue because you want to avoid having too many discontinued pieces on your sample boards that reps are showing to stores and that you cannot ship out. It is probably unavoidable to have some discontinued pieces on your sample boards at any given time, but you want to keep that number as low as possible.

Frequency of New Product Development

In apparel fashion, new product lines come out seasonally. There are new color pallets, new shapes, and new styles to think about. As a jewelry designer, you might think that it is a good idea to try and match your designs to what is coming out in the fashion world so you can more easily sell your collection to stores, and therefore believe that you have to come up with a new collection every season. Some very successful designers will come up with an entirely new collection every season, but this is by no means necessary for the average jewelry designer. Stores do like to see that you are creating new pieces and that your line is evolving, but this basically requires creating about 3 or 4 new boards (or about 15 to 20 new pieces) every 3 months.

Stores also do not all buy jewelry in the same season as they are currently in. In my experience, about half of apparel stores that carry jewelry do buy it for current sales, but the rest buy for 1-3 months in the future. Even if your collection is up to date with current trends, about half of the stores you try to sell to will be buying a season ahead. I recommend therefore not to worry about seasonality too much, in the sense that you do not necessarily need to be "on time" with your new creations. But you should think about "spring/summer" pallets and "fall/winter" pallets, in general, and you just never know when you will sell them.

Case Study: Dogeared

Dogeared is a brand of jewelry that sells small necklaces on paper cards with slogans that appeal to mass-market women such as "Karma" or "Three Wishes." Their pieces make great gifts and are extremely common to see both in stores and on people, if you know what to look for. Material cost for the type of small pendants the company makes, including packaging and labor, is probably under $5 in my personal estimation. The pieces retail for between $38 and $65 in department stores. I literally see people wearing these pieces on almost a daily basis and would venture to guess that the company is doing very well financially. This brand is a perfect example of having adopted a simple, small and super-salable jewelry design that capitalizes on mass-market trends and gets into almost every store.

Product Development and Design Tips

In all honesty, I am perplexed by the success of their simple designs and for a long time failed to understand why so many consumers would want to wear such non-descript pieces. But at the same time, I strongly respect their business acumen and must admit that I would not mind having that kind of success one bit! They seem to have their finger on the pulse of what the mass-market woman wants to buy and have managed to translate, through their packaging and brand messaging, tiny and simple geometric shapes into an emotion that so many women are buying consistently. Clearly, the simplicity of their jewelry has come to stand for the messages the brand emits and their strategy is working. Their style may not be for everyone, and it may not be for you, but the number of consumers they reach certainly makes them a viable case study for consideration.

The success of brands such as this one has made me contemplate and alter my jewelry strategy to include simpler, smaller pieces in my line. I wouldn't tell you that you need to do the same if your style is naturally more intricate, but at least knowing about a huge segment of the jewelry market that generates high-volume sales will be useful as you decide what direction your line will take.

Chapter 4

Creating Samples

Samples Explained

'Samples' are pieces of jewelry that are often affixed on sample boards and displayed as part of a cohesive collection showcasing your work. Samples are used for several different purposes, mainly for reps to carry on the road to show your line to stores. Along with being tools for reps, you might want to use samples to show your line to stores yourself. You can also use boards when are meeting with new reps - it is helpful if you have samples to show them. Reps will also use sample boards to display your line at tradeshows. It is good to know that if you are doing a tradeshow yourself, you will probably not use sample boards to display your pieces, but if you are being represented by a rep in the show, the rep will take your sample boards to use as displays.

Sample Boards

A sample board, or 'display pad', is a thin piece of fabric-upholstered board of specific dimension, almost always 14-1/8"W x 7-5/8"D. You affix your jewelry to sample boards in order to display your line. The main types of sample boards, by material, are velvet, faux-suede, leatherette, and cotton or synthetic fabric. They come in a huge array of colors and cost anywhere from 99 cents to seven dollars per board, depending on the type and quality of the fabric lining, as well as the quantity you're purchasing. The type of fabric lining and colors that you use are ultimately up to you and what you feel will go best with your jewelry designs, but there are certain things to watch out for.

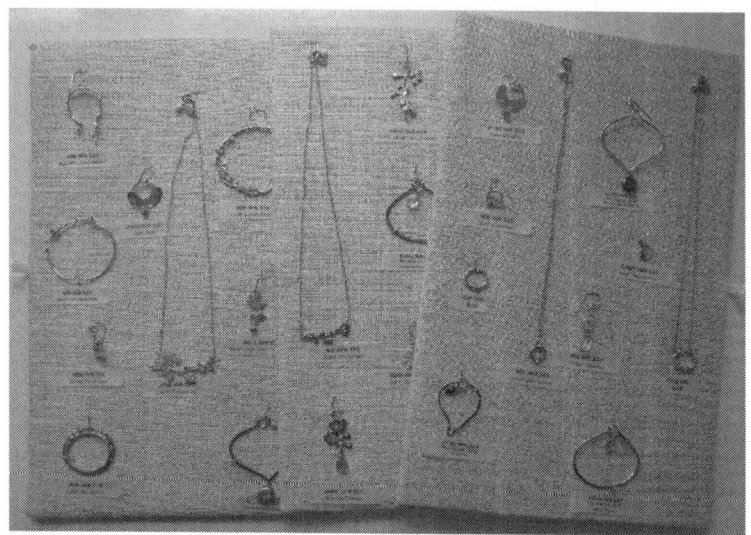

Efy Tal Sample Boards

The most commonly-used type of sample board, that you will invariably encounter everywhere, is a black velvet board. I find black velvet to be a very poor choice, despite its mainstream adoption, for several reasons. Black is a very harsh color against most jewelry and tends to attract dust and all manner of particles. Even if your boards look good when you first make them, they experience wear and tear much more quickly than other color/fabric combinations, plus make your boards look old and dirty fast. I also do not recommend using cheap (99 cent) faux-suede boards, in any color, because those boards do not hold pins down well and they will pop out. This makes the jewelry slide around, which is very frustrating for reps.

As an alternative to black, I like using beige-toned fabrics. Beige tends to look simple, yet expensive, and usually allow the jewelry to shine. However, if you tend to have only very small, thin pieces in your line, you may want to avoid beige because your jewelry might fade against the background and generally not be very visible. You can get sample boards at the following locations: Nilecorp.com, firemountaingems.com, jewelrydisplay.com and RioGrande.com

In order to put your sample boards together, you buy 'u-pins', which are small, u-shaped pins that you use to hold your jewelry down on the sample boards. These come in both gold and silver, so you can match them to the type of jewelry you are displaying. You can get u-pins at www.jewelrydisplay.com. There is no substitute for using u-pins, so do not even try to use any other kind. Nothing will pin down your jewelry as securely and neatly. In order to correctly display earrings, I suggest actually poking the ear wire directly into the fabric of your sample boards, because any other method you try will not allow them to lay flat.

You want to make sure that you use lots of u-pins to affix your jewelry to the boards for two reasons. Firstly, you want to make sure that the jewelry will not move around when being transported or displayed in different positions. Secondly, the more u-pins are on a piece of jewelry and, therefore, the more difficult a piece of jewelry is to take off the board and try on, the less likely store owners are to ask to try on every piece from your collection. This creates a huge mess because reps will not take the time to carefully re-arrange all of the samples on your boards like you had them originally.

Once you pin your jewelry to the boards, you will want to label each piece with its style number and wholesale price. This makes taking orders seamless and reduces confusion and time-wasting since stores can quickly see your prices and reps can quickly take down orders. When reps have to look up styles and prices later from a book or website, the risk of getting orders wrong greatly increases. You will also want to put any special stones you are using or special meaning behind the jewelry on the labels since buyers are always looking for a hook.

Labeling Jewelry on a Sample Board

All of the labeling described above needs to be professional and typed for each individual piece of jewelry. Going to tradeshows showed me that labels *really* need to be typed, small, and neat. Hand-written labels and bell-shaped ID tags really do not look professional and will not blend in with other designers' displays. In addition to looking unattractive, these labels will constantly come off of your boards and tangle with your jewelry.

For light colored sample boards, I use clear return address labels from Avery (product number 15667), which you can buy at any office supply retail location or on Amazon. These labels are made to be for return addresses, but happen to work really well on sample boards. You can program your word processor to use the template of the boxes (use Avery template number 5167) so that you are typing into the boxes of the labels when you print them. If you are using a darker colored board, you will likely want to use white labels.

Although these labels have adhesive on the back, they will have a tendency to come off unless you supplement the adhesive with glue. I recommend picking strong glue, like Scotch superglue, which is a clear drying and that comes out of a tube so that you can neatly dot it on. Keep in mind that using glue to affix your labels will make it such that, when it is time to change up your collection and reuse your sample boards, you will be left with some glue residue. It is then up to you whether or not you want to reuse the boards or buy new ones. But, the glue definitely is a must.

No matter what you do, and despite best efforts, jewelry pieces and labels still fall off or get separated from the sample boards. Then reps neither know nor have the inclination to figure out where to put them back. But, here's a special insider sample board tip that works well, but almost nobody does: always take a picture of the board layout, print it out, and paste it to the back of the board! With a picture, you have not only a re-creation of your entire board, but you will also facilitate reps making notes on the pictures such as sales talking points, or changes in materials/price that you made.

Another great tip to make sure that your sample boards look good for a long time is to send to your reps, once it is clear that they are keeping your line, the best kind of tarnish remover. I use Empire Instant Tarnish Remover (pink solution) which I get at OttoFrei.com. This will encourage them to clean your pieces, since you provide the product, and keep them looking shiny and new for appointments. Lastly, while you may be breaking sample boards apart after use, if you take pictures, you can store them in your files in case you ever want to bring back a certain collection, mini-collection, or need to remember how you configured certain combinations in the past. You can also use these pictures in your style look-up book for your employees, but more on that in a later chapter.

Taking pictures will, of course, increase the time, effort, and cost of putting together your sample boards, but believe me, it is well worth it. Including pictures will make you your rep's favorite line, because you are making their job easier. It will also increase their motivation to treat your samples with respect and make sure that your boards always look like the picture. This, in turn, increases your sales, because there is a direct correlation between how professional your samples look and how much of your jewelry gets sold.

Sample Selection and Editing

To have a complete collection, you want to have about 20 finished sample boards, with about 5-8 pieces on each board. This would make a complete collection of around 100 samples. Each board, or board grouping, should have a story or a theme that ties the pieces together. You want to look for similar design elements, colors, or inspiration behind the pieces to group them together in a way that makes sense.

If you are starting from scratch, it will seem that coming up with 100 pieces is a monumental task. While this is true for the beginning jewelry designer, most designers who have been creating for a while have hundreds of pieces to choose from when putting together a cohesive collection. The main challenge becomes editing a collection out of their large stock of jewelry.

When editing down for a collection, you want to make sure you have some eye-catching 'signature pieces' that really represent your unique vision, but also a good mix of basic pieces, since those are the ones that tend to sell with higher frequency. You want to group these pieces together into mini-collections of a couple of boards. Each mini-collection can consist of anywhere from one board, or 5-8 pieces of jewelry, to five boards, 25 to 40 pieces. You want to keep making cohesive mini-collections of between one to five boards, mixing both unique signature pieces and basic pieces into each mini-collection, until you have achieved the desired number of about 20 completed boards.

Line Sheets

Line sheets are basically thumbnail images of each of your products with style number and wholesale price written right below the picture. They are primarily used for stores to re-order and for reps to leave with stores or hand out at tradeshows. Line sheets should ideally consist of about 20 images per page. The quality of the images and the printing on line sheets does not need to be the highest quality, but the pictures should be neatly tiled onto the page so as to look professional. Therefore, if you do not have high-quality pictures, or do not want to spend money on professional ones, you can get away with more basic pictures for line sheets, as long as the finished product looks neat and professional. If you have some professional images, such as for your website, along with images that you take yourself, you're welcome to use both on the sheet. To arrange the pictures correctly, you can use Photoshop, Gimp (which is free), or

Creating Samples

PicMonkey.com (my favorite, free / cheap and super easy with ready made collage and grid templates) or you can hire a graphic designer, if you have the resources.

Efy Tal Line Sheets

Taking some of the stress out of selling, line sheets also do not have to be professionally bound, they can simply be stapled together and can also be printed double-sided to save costs. Because line sheets can be extremely time-consuming to create and need constant updating, I would not let making them be a show-stopper in terms of getting your line out the door. However, most designers do have them and once reps get your samples they will start asking for line sheets. A little tip: you can negotiate prices with your local print shop, so never assume you will be charged the advertised price for printing. You will find yourself ordering many, many copies to send out, so print shops will be happy to work with you to make sure you come back for future printings.

Line sheets can be somewhat of a double-edged sword. On the one hand, they can be used for easy re-ordering by stores. On the other hand, some stores use the fact that they have your line sheets to avoid appointments with your rep. It is always best for stores to see your rep face-to-face, because those who say they can reorder off of the line sheet often don't, or they order less than they would after a face-to-face appointment. It is therefore crucial to understand that sending out line sheets does not replace a rep or live appointments.

Reps are also often apprehensive to give out line sheets at tradeshows because buyers will sometimes grab the line sheets instead of scheduling a meeting to go through the line. This, of course, results in fewer sales and is also wasteful. You should discuss this with your rep in advance of any tradeshows at which they might represent you and agree in advance as to whom gets line sheets, making it clear that they should not simply leave them sitting out at the booth.

A final cautionary note about line sheets is that, if acquired by the wrong people, they can be used to copy your line. This is, to a certain extent, unavoidable, since you will ideally have pictures of your jewelry circulating online and many other places, but be mindful of both your costs and this potential for copying when you decide where, when, and to whom you give your sheets. Big jewelry lines who are trying to set trends often do not put pictures of their lines up on their websites until buyers have seen the lines, precisely to avoid this kind of copying.

Chapter 5

Branding and Marketing

In an ideal world, you will have your logo, your colors, your fonts, and any other major design themes well thought-out before you begin printing your marketing materials. Ideally, common design themes should run throughout all of your marketing materials, including your website and all of your print and packaging. Consistent brand messaging will give buyers the feeling that your line is mature, put-together, and will allow you to command your price point with greater authority, legitimizing your brand in the eyes of the consumer.

Having said this, I feel it is important to note that, even after being in the jewelry business for seven years, my brand and marketing materials are still evolving. If you wait until you are sure that all of your materials represent your brand in the best possible way, you will be waiting a very long time to launch your line. While I do want to emphasize the importance of coming up with a consistent branding and marketing scheme, I do not want to insinuate that you should be paralyzed from beginning your activities until you are 100% sure of your success . Do your best to come up with branding elements you think you will be able to use across products and over time, but do not be surprised if your vision changes.

Branding and Marketing

Designing a Logo

A logo should ideally be the kind of image that any person can look at for a second, close their eyes, and be able to visualize. There should be something memorable about your logo and it should be unique to your brand, making customers think of you whenever they see it. Because of the importance of a logo, and the fact that you ideally want to include it on everything you put out, from your business cards to your website to your line sheets, etc., you will want your logo to be perfect. Your logo will be on everything you create and you should dedicate the highest percentage of your marketing development time to its creation.

Coming up with a perfect logo is a daunting task even for marketing and graphic design professionals that create them for a living. If you happen to be very graphically inclined, great! But if you are not, understand that you could potentially spend an infinite amount of time perfecting your logo, and many people do. That is to be expected. All you can do when you are first designing a logo is spend a reasonable amount of time on it, come up with something that you think is memorable, unique, and attractive, share it with people to get their opinion, tweak as necessary, and then just go with it. Your vision might change in the future and you may create a different logo in the future. Though that is not optimal, in happens and is fine.

Taking Professional Pictures

Professional pictures should be used for your website, selling in other online forums, your look-book, and for showing your line to reps and stores. By professional pictures, what I mean is a very high standard of photographic quality that can usually only be achieved by a professional photographer (i.e., usually not you, unless you are a professional photographer). Professional photographers have high-grade, expensive cameras, expensive lighting solutions and other equipment, and tremendous know-how regarding achieving professional photographs.

Though I have taken some nice pictures on my own, there was no comparison. The professional's were simply much better. Yet, there are always exceptions to the rule. According to their Facebook page, the team at http://www.spiffingjewelry.com/ says they take their pictures themselves on top of a microwave with different color paper, next to a window, so apparently it can be done. I think their pictures are great and simple, take a look.

Whether or not your pictures look professional enough to use for your line is a subjective question. But the point regarding professionalism is, if customers are looking at the pictures and they look like they could possibly have been taken at home by an amateur, then they are not professional enough. You want pictures of your jewelry to represent your creations and your brand in the best possible light. You want to look like the professional jewelry designer that you aspire to be. The bottom line is, do not skimp on pictures.

As a note, even if you happen to be a great photographer, you will know that taking professional-grade pictures is extremely time consuming. Therefore, even if you could take them yourself, you could probably be using this time to strategically work on your business rather than creating perfect pictures. Unless you are really a professional photographer, just hire one.

If you try to find a professional photographer online without knowing where to look, you will normally see very high hourly fees of around $30-$40 per image which is unaffordable for most beginning designers. However, there are less expensive routes. The best way to find a photographer is to target people who just graduated from photography programs, have technical training, and are looking to make a name for themselves. To target these people, place an ad on Craigslist or at a photography program advertising that you are looking for professional-grade pictures by a photographer who specializes in jewelry and apparel, that you are willing to pay about $2 per picture, and that you are looking to commission hundreds of photographs on an ongoing basis.

If you cannot find anyone to answer your ad, there are two more options. You can increase the $2 per picture to a maximum of $4 per picture, but you really shouldn't go beyond that price. You will realize that photography is such a large cost of business and that you will need so many pictures over time that it is really worth working hard to find a good photographer who will stick to these prices. You can always start with one photographer while continuing your search for the perfect photographer. Another option, if you live in an expensive city, is to post ads in less expensive parts of the country. You can send a photographer who lives in a different city or state a few samples of jewelry, test out the pictures, and develop a remote relationship. I have seen this remote option work quite well.

When a photographer agrees to photograph your jewelry for about $2 - $4 per piece, you will have to expect to receive dozens, or even hundreds, of images with the same background and setup, or images against a plain white background. You may incidentally need white background images for certain websites anyway, like Amazon. You cannot expect the photographer to create a whole setup, backdrop, and lighting scheme for each piece of jewelry. Though, you will have to agree on a few setups that you like and agree to receive most of your pictures that way. Otherwise, it is impossible to make the $2 - $4 per image pricing practicable.

It goes without saying that this pricing range does not include so-called 'money shots', which are specialized, artistic images that you might use for the home page of your website or the cover of your look book. For money shots, you should expect to pay somewhere around $4 - $10 an image, if choose to work with the same photographer you're using for the rest of your pictures. You will need a few money shots in addition to your

Branding and Marketing

larger portfolio of photographs, which should include every piece in your collection.

Lastly, you may want to include some 'model shots' of models wearing your jewelry. Model shots are by far the most expensive kind of picture to commission. For just a close-up shot of a necklace on a neck or an earring on an ear, you should expect the same price as other images - the $2-$4 per shot, plus the cost of the model. For shots that include the model's face and/or full body, you should expect to pay around $15-$20 per shot, plus the cost of the model, because these shots take so much time to set up and perfect, due to the added complication of capturing a good shot of the model along with highlighting your jewelry.

Tags (Metal and Cardboard) and Earring Cards

Tags are little pieces of metal or cardboard featuring your brand name that you attach to all of your jewelry and marketing materials. This way, people can trace your products back to you and find you in the future. I use both metal tags and cardboard tags on my jewelry. I add small metal tags on the back of my chains, like on necklaces and bracelets, by the closing clasp. My metal tags are small ovals with the name "Efy" stamped in my signature font.

A metal tag should be very small, since it should fit nicely next to the chain clasp without overwhelming it or making the item bulky. Therefore, you can choose to put a small logo on it or, if your brand name is short like mine, the name. I also use my metal stamp to affix my name on the back of my original designs.

My Logo Stamped To The Back Of My Jewelry

To create metal tags, you can get your own custom stamp created for you, for example through www.infinitystamps.com or RioGrande, and stamp each of your tags yourself. Or, better yet, you can create one original tag using clay metal and then get your tags cast. If you get your tags cast, you can budget about 25¢ –75¢ per tag depending on material, quantity, and manufacturer. I would never pay more. If you need an original font or logo, you will have to have an original stamp made from an image. Here, for example, is my metal tag:

Branding and Marketing

Efy Jewelry Metal Tag on Back of Necklaces

Conversely, a cardboard tag is a small piece of cardboard with your full brand name and logo on it. I attach these onto the back of necklaces also, and these can be used to place prices on. Beware that these cardboard tags are not cheap, you can budget around 25¢ per cardboard tag. Many store owners may take these off of your items before displaying them if they do not want to promote your brand directly, but you should still try to include them wherever makes sense to advertise your line and make it as easy as you can for customers to find you. I get my cardboard tags at Dolphin Bead Design - www.dolphinbead.com.

Efy Tal Cardboard Tag on Back of Necklaces

Earring cards are a display mechanism you are probably already familiar with. They are small cardboard cards with little holes in them to display and sell earrings on. I also get my earring cards from Dolphin Bead Design and they run about 50¢ per card. In my opinion, these cards are appropriate for earrings under $50. If your earrings are more expensive than that, earring cards may cheapen the look, so opt for another method of display.

Since earring cards are not cheap, you will want to make sure that you do not give out your earrings on earring cards to stores that do not intend to display them with that setup. Many stores will actually insist that you present your earrings on earring cards, since that is the only way they will display, but you should double-check before sending them. One quick note about earring cards: the generic plastic earring cards with the little bent edge for

Branding and Marketing

display should be avoided. If you can, make your own custom earring cards with your own brand name and logo on them. They are a much more professional, expensive-looking, and personal way to present your earrings and another good differentiator of your brand. I get mine made at www.dolphinbead.com also.

Developing Your Story

I have heard time and time again that having a story behind your brand sells product. Of course, the more unique and captivating your story, the more it will help drive sales. But, if you

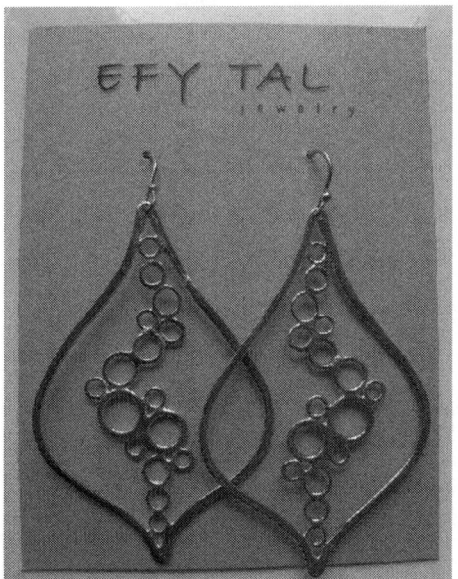

Efy Tal Earring Cards

do not have an amazing story naturally ready to tell, take time to figure one out. You can start by reading the 'About Us' section of other designers' websites that you admire and take tips. You will be using your story very often, so you should have it straight. The story will certainly be published on your website, but stores, sales staff and reps will also ask for your story so that they can educate their customers about your line. Your story should also appear on all of your more comprehensive print materials.

Every designer has a different story. There are no necessary elements to a story *per se*, but you want to describe what inspires you. You should take time to think of a good answer to the question: "what is your main inspiration?" Almost every person you come across in the jewelry world will ask you. For example, Pyrrha Jewelry was able to take old wax seals, each of which have a meaning and were family heirlooms from a grandfather, and use them as inspiration for a jewelry line. This is a great example of a brand's story because **customers love finding deeper meanings behind designs!** Can you say, honestly, that you didn't find the story behind the wax seals interesting on some level?

As another example, the Jes Maharry line tells the story about how the founder, Jes, grew up with horses in a free-spirited family of artists. She still lives with horses, which became her creative inspiration. There are also many designers, such as Nashelle, who talk about how they started their lines while being a mother to 4 boys. This family angle is also a great one to share with women. Your story can be about the jewelry itself, like if it's made out of recycled something or other, or say if you donate a portion of sales to charity, or you employ homeless people - you get the idea.

For my own line, I concentrate on jewelry-related anecdotes when relaying my story and do not simply tell my life progression. Though I was an engineer for many years and underwent a drastic career change, this is not what I use as my brand's story. Your brand story might be different than your life story. Ultimately, it should center on creative and, ideally, jewelry-related anecdotes.

What I concentrate on telling in my brand's story are the true facts of my jewelry-obsessed childhood: how I used to go to school with a ring on every finger and long, dangly earrings hidden in my backpack so my mother would not find them. How my obsession with jewelry started at an early age and I was able to hone my taste and skills throughout the years. Mine is not necessarily the most compelling of stories, but it gets the job done. You will have to come up with something similar - at least a somewhat unique and justifiable reason for your brand's existence.

Shelf Talkers and Brand Markers

A 'shelf talker' is a small cardboard or framed display, such as a folded greeting card, that is well designed and printed by a professional printing service, such as VistaPrint. It should be large enough to be a visible centerpiece next to your jewelry items in a store and also to fit your printed story. Here is my first shelf talker from years ago:

Another piece of advertising or brand messaging that most

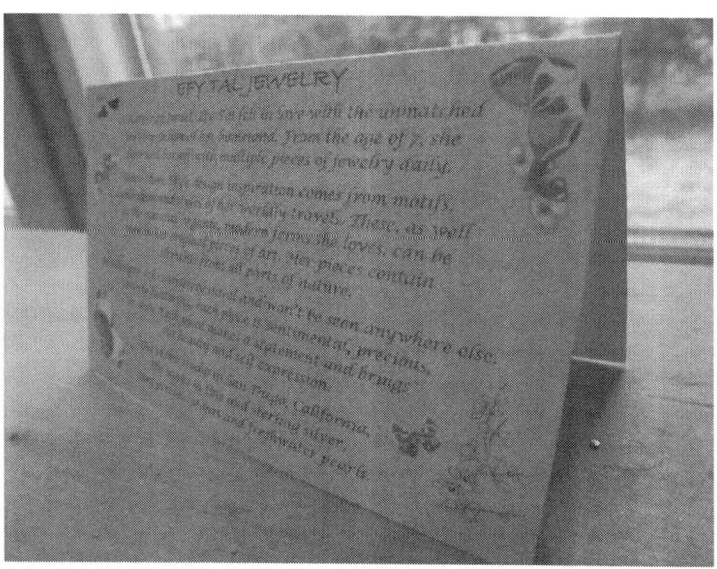

My First Shelf Talker

stores will happily display is a more permanent fixture called a 'brand marker'. This is usually a physical, tangible item with your brand name and logo on it. It can be an engraved crystal, in many cases, or an engraved river-rock, which I use. You can also use a miniature picture frame with a small card in it.

Branding and Marketing

If you order many brand markers at a time, you can get them for as cheaply as $3 each. But, unless you order by the hundreds as I do, you should plan on spending about $5-$8 per piece. Be careful because it is easy to overspend on brand markers, and there are certainly companies that will charge much more than I would recommend spending. I buy my river-rock brand markers from Engraved Stones Direct (www.engravedstonesdirect.com). Here is my brand marker:

Efy Tal Brand Makers

Look-Book

A look-book is a great way to get in the door with stores which does not require you to have an appointment with the stores' buyers. It is usually very difficult to get buyer appointments, since they are always busy and somewhat skeptical of new lines. You can use the look-book to get through the door of a new account and reps can also pull it out during appointments when they are showing other lines, even if they could not get an appointment to show your line, which makes for easy extra access to new stores.

For a look-book, you really want to have incredible quality images and printing. As always, think very professional product. A look-book is also a great place to include your story, if you happen to have a good one, because buyers are always looking for a hook. You should also include any selling points you might have, such as the meaning behind the jewelry, if you're "Made in the USA", and possibly listing the materials you use. Lastly, and this may go without saying, you should definitely include all of your contact information, website, email, fax, phone, etc.

Efy Tal Original Look Book

Branding and Marketing

A look-book does not have to be long. You can have anywhere between 10 - 30 images inside. Of course, as you get more established and grow your budget, you will want to have all of your shots on models, in which the models can wear multiple pieces of jewelry in each image. As a good example, search for Vanessa Mooney's look-book on their website. However, if you are just starting out, images of the jewelry is enough. It would be ideal if you could photograph the jewelry next to some object, such as a flower or other attractive item, to give it scale and enhance the interest of the image.

A look-book should be bound, not stapled, unlike a line sheet. You will ideally be using high-quality paper, photographs, and printing, so you should do everything you can to make the look-book look highly professional. You can get the look-book bound, spiral or stitch, at any copy center. Alternatively, less expensive than binding, but still looking decently professional, is having a nice folder and placing your high quality look-book sheets inside, loose-leaf. This is not as desirable an option as binding, but it looks much better than stapling. Of course, as soon as you get your gorgeous look book off the press, it will be time to start working on your next one!

While they may not make the time for an appointment, buyers may casually flip through the look-book and some pieces might catch their eye. For this reason, you will want to include style numbers in your look-book because buyers might decide that they want to order from you right away. (Wouldn't that be great?!) It is important that they be able to place an order easily using the look-book. You should also therefore include a price list on a separate sheet that you can easily switch out as you get new books printed.

Website

A complete website is not necessarily where a new jewelry designer should put all of their time and energy when putting together a line. To create a complete, professional website that displays all of your products can take months and is a huge undertaking. However, it is a good idea to have a basic one as an online representation of you.

I will not describe the different website platforms or how to design a website, because there is already a vast amount of literature on the subject. Today, making a website is extremely easy technically, but it is very time consuming in terms of uploading pictures of your entire inventory and writing good copy, plus it is costly to develop a database of pictures that are professional enough to put up. What I would recommend for a starting jewelry designer is having a simple website that you use basically as an online brochure for your line that allows people to find you, see who you are, and get in contact with you for orders. The website should contain at least 10 - 30 images, which, similarly to the look-book, is just about enough to give buyers a good idea of your line so they will grant you an appointment.

Branding and Marketing

Your website should, of course, contain your ordering contact information so that you can refer people to it easily and they can find what they need to get in touch with you to place orders.

As you start being able to upload more and more images of products, you can start to turn your website into an e-commerce site to make sales directly from the page. You should know that some reps will frown upon you having an e-commerce site and will not use it as a tool for getting appointments, and stores may also refuse to sell your products because customers can get your jewelry directly from you online. If you are set on having an e-commerce site, you should not let this restriction discourage you, because pretty much no rep or store can give you enough loyalty or business to be worth the sales you could ultimately generate online. However, if you are far from being able to generate and efficiently fill online orders, you might want to delay going the e-commerce route.

Selling directly to customers through your website is a very difficult operation as it takes a lot of work to make your site easy to find and to generate a high volume of online traffic. You are not going to generate sales until you already have a following and people are seeing your jewelry all over the place. You could put yourself in a position where you waste a lot of time and money developing the perfect website, but because you have not developed other sales avenues and customers, your site will sit idle. Therefore, I would not waste a lot of energy trying to make your website an e-commerce site until you are functionally running in every other way. The best beginner website gives users a flavor of your line and your contact information so that you can process orders. Just a note: my website did not actually start generating serious income for years. Though, they increased dramatically when I switched to shopify.com as my platform.

One additional note is that, if you are already sure that you want to have an e-commerce site, before embarking on building it, you should take some time to research the different web platforms, because moving a complete website from one platform to another is extremely time consuming and disruptive to your business.

What you should aim for once you have a basic website running, is enabling orders from preexisting store accounts to come in through your site and a secure log-in. This is different than trying to appeal to and fill orders from strangers around the world. What you can do, once you have all of your photography and images uploaded onto the site along with style numbers and prices, is create a password-protected section of the site that is accessible only to your regular accounts. They should be able to log onto the site and enter their orders themselves. Most platforms support this, but make sure before you decide on one. This is a great way to generate some hands free income from stores that you've had a long running relationship with. New stores will also periodically contact you and ask to make wholesale purchases with you directly.

Also, once all of your products are uploaded onto your site on a routine basis, you can use your website as a convenient database for your employees to look up jewelry by style number. That way, if you or your employees see an order for a piece of jewelry and need an efficient way to look it up, they can enter the style number into the website and be able to see a detailed picture of the item, its price, and any relevant materials information. Of course, this database will only be useful if you enter all of your styles onto the website and update it regularly. If you do not have professional-quality pictures for this part of the website, that is ok. You can put up lower-quality pictures of items that are inactive and searchable only by you and your employees to fulfill this database function.

Social Media

While it is understandably an important topic, I won't discuss social media in depth because there are so many books on the topic and because the landscape of social media changes so quickly that once you read this book the information in this section might be obsolete. My favorite book right now on this topic is by social media expert Gary Vaynerchuck called *Jab Jab Jab Right Hook*. This is a **must read**. I am sadly very late to the social media party and it is one of my biggest regrets. Now I'm on a treadmill that I can barely get off of to devote the time required. Nonetheless, we'll be adding a social media person to our team to help us out. Don't make the mistake I have made and undermine the importance of this, especially if you're over 25 and are not grasping the significance of this media form. Let me make a few points regarding social media from the book and my experience:

1) Social media is not an option. This is a **must** for any serious brand, and it will really help your business if done right.

2) Whatever social media channels you choose to use, be it Facebook, Instagram, Pinterest, etc., you will wish you had started sooner! Time is your friend here and there is no substitute for it to build quality followers. Try to get your social media functions up and working as soon as possible. If nothing else, open accounts, put up a picture with all your information, and let these start to build organically right away. When you get your act together (hopefully sooner rather than later) start updating on a regular basis with a certain methodology in mind.

3) You have to be native – meaning each social media platform has its own style, slang, format, and reason for being. You cannot use the same posts across all platforms. You need to be familiar with each platform by spending a good amount of time on each one and reading up on them before you can start posting on them.

4) You need to give, and keep giving, free content that your followers find fascinating, engaging, funny, thought provoking, educational, and they want to share with their friends. Only ask for something (promotion, visit new collection, etc.) rarely.

5) Your fans want to see effort, that you are speaking to them within a context, and that it's not just an afterthought for you. So this requires a lot of effort, time, and dedication. You may need to hire somebody to do this, or know that this is one of the activities that will you will need to dedicate plenty of time for.

6) Be prepared to give away lots of jewelry. Social media is a great way to generate traffic to your websites, the stores you're in, and is a must for your brand development. It also helps create loyal repeat customers who feel like they know you.

7) There are some great tools out there to help you create amazing images very easily and inexpensively with professional looking text, effects, overlays, watermarks, logos, borders, collages, links (my favorite is www.PicMonkey.com). For videos use www.camtasia-studio.com, and for infographics use infogr.am.

Press

It is a common misconception that if you want your line to succeed you should get celebrities to wear your jewelry or that you need to have your line featured in magazines and blogs. This requires sending hundreds of samples to celebrities or their agents in the hopes that they might be seen wearing your jewelry and, ideally, photographed in it, as well as signing up with PR firms to get into magazines. This assumes that you actually have the addresses of the relevant celebrities and PR people that will get your jewelry seen. Realistically, most people do not have access to these exclusive lists, and therefore end up sending their jewelry in random, dead-end directions in the hopes that someone will know someone who knows someone that will get their jewelry into the right hands. The odds of a celebrity actually being photographed in your jewelry and your brand being identified in a story are slim to none, unless you really have the right connections from the start. Even if that happens, and you post that picture on your website, if you yourself don't have much traffic then no one will see these images.

The first problem with the celebrity approach to press is that, even in the best case scenario, if someone is photographed in your jewelry and you end up in an article, you might see a small spike in your sales, but this is not a sustainable business model. You could easily spend thousands of dollars on this marketing strategy and, in all likelihood, nothing will come of it, so do not invest in this strategy unless you have virtually unlimited funds, or prestige is more important to you than a healthy business.

If you do have some disposable funds, they would be much better spent hiring people to do the parts of your business that you want automated to free up your time to concentrate on growing your business. But, if you really want to pursue having celebrities photographed in your jewelry, the way to go about this most reliably is to get hold of their stylists. To find stylists, look for styling credits in magazines or in industry guides such as Le Book. Your best bet in this arena, however, would be to send the celebrity management (the public information that is on their website) a gift with a personalized note for the celebrity and hope that they send you a shout-out on their social media page(s) where many people will see it.

If you want to attract some press without spending a lot of money, then develop a very compelling brand story that people will want to hear, as we discussed previously. Magazine editors look for interesting content for their readers, too, and your story cannot just be a plug for your line. It has to be truly compelling in order to get published. Most people do not have such compelling brand stories, but if you do, you can send them to magazine and blog editors to see if you get traction. Just be aware that this is also very time consuming and you may see little return on your time investment.

What is unquestionably worthwhile, no matter what press avenues you will pursue in the future, is to invest in a good look-book, or at least exceptional images. The time and money you invest in a professional, beautiful look-book will be the best press you can create for your brand. If you decide you want to pursue printed press in a traditional magazine, the first step is sending your look-book to magazine editors, along with a relevant piece of news, and the look-book will do most of your talking for you.

For mainstream fashion magazines, you will want to contact them at least 4 months ahead of time or you will be too late to get into the issue you want. At such magazines, you should generally contact one editor and not more, since they confer regarding the stories they will publish. If an editor likes your look-book and thinks your line is appropriate for a feature, they might agree to meet with you to present samples in person. If your line is not appropriate for the stories being run at the time that you submit, a good look-book will ensure that the magazine keeps your line on file and contacts you in the future.

For shorter-lead publications such as blogs, you do not need to give as much notice as for print publications. In my opinion, blogs are actually the best bang for your buck in terms of press. They require much less of your time to get accepted onto a blog, less notice than with print publications, there are many more blogs than print publications, and many important fashion blogs are attracting large numbers of readers. Of course traditional magazines carry a different sort of prestige, so ultimately each designer has to make their own calculation with regard to which press outlets to target.

The bottom line with press is I do not recommend going above and beyond trying to get traditional printed press or high-profile, celebrity press, hiring PR firms and so on for most designers. I recommend social media and blogs, which you can read about extensively in tutorials on marketing and press, and of course having a great, well-maintained website and look book. But each designer should make their own calculations on the basis of their connections and means, both time and money, to devote to press.

Chapter 6

Production

Manufacturing

Manufacturing jewelry basically involves casting or 'fabrication', or creating each piece from scratch, of your pieces and then assembling them. What I have found works for me is to outsource my casting and do my assembly in-house, but this is not the only way to do it. However, there are 2 reasons that this works well. The first is that it allows me to have my jewelry studio in my house. I don't need as much equipment as if I was doing my own casting and/or fabrication and all of the work done in the house is safe. The second is that each piece takes about 10 minutes to assemble in-house, as opposed to the hours it could potentially take to cast or fabricate, so I feel that the casting is a worthwhile delegation.

The challenge with getting manufacturers to cast your pieces is that each factory has different capabilities. For instance, most factories will not set stones, some factories will not do certain types of plating and finishes, some will not use certain metals, some do not have a good pricing structure for small pieces, etc. So your first challenge will be finding a factory, or factories, that meet your business needs and are able to fill your orders at a reasonable price. It is very difficult to find a good factory, get in contact with them, and do consistent business. Most factories will end up not meeting your needs, for one reason or another, and it is easy to get disappointed or discouraged. But do not feel discouraged, you will eventually find the right fit.

A note about personalities: if you are the type of person who expects that when someone gives you their word they will keep it, and that you can count on people to get things done when they say they will, you will have to drastically re-adjust this expectation when it comes to dealing with factories. That is, if you want to keep any hairs on your head.

Having an ongoing relationship with people at a factory is absolutely essential. It is a necessary, but not sufficient, component of a successful operation. That means that, just because you have a good relationship with someone at a factory does not mean that the factory will not disappoint you. But, you do need to cultivate relationships with people at factories in order to have even a shot at getting anything done. You should cultivate multiple connections because you cannot just depend on one factory. When one is unable to fulfill your needs, you will need to be able to quickly move to someone else with the order.

You have various options with respect to manufacturing, both in the U.S. and overseas. One resource for finding manufacturers is by visiting the MAGIC show in Las Vegas, which is a fashion and accessories trade show for buyers. There is a large section of the show dedicated to 'sourcing', which has hundreds of factory representatives from all over the world and country, as well as presentations from experts teaching about sourcing and working with factories, plus hundreds of other topics. This would be very worthwhile for any serious designer. Visit http://www.magiconline.com/sourcing-at-magic. We'll touch more on tradeshows in a later chapter.

In the U.S.

In the U.S., the major manufacturers are located in Los Angeles and New York, although there are other local operations. Many cities/counties have a 'jewelry exchange' where you can get pieces made, but those tend to be quite expensive because there is not a lot of competition in the local markets. To start finding good U.S. factories, you may want to actually go on-site to some of the major jewelry areas and explore the factories in person.

In Los Angeles, the jewelry district is centered around Hill Street. Just about every building on, and just off, that street houses jewelry manufacturers. On the main floor there are all the retailers. On the higher levels, these are all factories of every size/type. There are, therefore, hundreds of jewelry manufacturers concentrated in a very small area.

New York's jewelry district is mostly centered around 47th street between 5th and 6th Avenue, as well as on 48th and some other streets nearby. In New York, unfortunately, the casters are different from the finishers, who are different from the 'platers', so a lot of coordination is required. There are even agents who can do all of this coordination for you, for a nominal fee. Ask the factories to recommend names.

Again, you will notice that the first floors of the buildings are usually storefronts that sell jewelry like in LA, though they

Production

often sell diamonds. The factories that cast the jewelry are usually located in the higher-up floors of these same buildings. Not all of the store-keepers will know where the factories are, but some will. I found factories by literally walking from storefront to storefront and asking for contacts. Once you build a list of contacts and meet with factories, you can maintain relationships with them remotely, from wherever you live. Of course, if you already have access to a list of factories, or if you happen to have your own contacts, you can build relationships with the factories remotely too by sending in some sample pieces to cast and giving them a try. I'm currently working on compiling a list of factories. You can always contact me at info@YourOwnJewelryLine.com if you're interested in such a list.

Another way to find factories in the U.S. is to go to your local gem show or Gem Faire, where you can buy pre-made castings by the hundreds. There you can ask the vendors who sell the castings if they will cast your pieces for you. They will often be happy to take your original pieces and have them cast for you using their network because they take a small cut of the cost.

My favorite option for finding factories for castings is actually online. Etsy.com has a huge list of suppliers on it and, while many factories are not yet on Etsy, many folks who deal with factories have opened up shops there. While the owners of these factories are often traditional and old-school, their kids are often modernizing their businesses and getting them online. The result is that there are literally hundreds of casting factories and agents that you can now find online by searching through the Etsy supplier lists.

Overseas

To find factories overseas, there are two main options. The first one is, similarly to the domestic option, to go abroad in person. You can Google agents that will put you in contact with factories if you are taking a trip. In each city, town, or village where the factory-houses are located, you usually have middle-men and agents whose job is to connect you.

The factories are mainly located in Thailand, Indonesia, Mexico, India, China, and South Korea. Regardless of where you go or who you are dealing with, unless it is an agent specialized in working with customers from abroad, expect that English will not be the main language of business and that communication with factories abroad can be very challenging.

While manufacturing overseas can provide a new level of price breaks, there are many challenges that come along with it and it is not for the faint of heart. One of the main problems is the cultural differences. For example, in most of these countries, people don't speak directly and clearly. If they can't do something, or simply don't want to do it, they will not say 'no'. They will either not respond, or will say 'yes' and will string you along for weeks or months. If they lose your original piece, they will often not admit it, they will just avoid the issue for months until you figure out what happened. It is also very common for them to not respect women and not conduct business with you the way you are used to be treated. I've already mentioned that what factories say they will do has no relation to what they will actually do. Working with middle men is only slightly helpful with these matters because they are normally part of the same culture and they have no intention of taking any personal loss if anything goes wrong.

Some of the other challenges are what you might imagine: sending samples back and forth can be costly, packages can be caught in customs for a long time, and you're also required to get very large quantities. In Thailand and Indonesia, for sterling silver, the quantity might be 50 - 100 minimum. In China, the minimums are 300 - 1000, usually 1000. If there is a problem with your production, they won't take the merchandise back; the most you can hope for is a 10% discount. No matter how much you order, you are likely to be their smallest and most insignificant client, so be prepared to be treated that way. Also be prepared to be knocked off, i.e. have cheaper versions of your designs made and sold. That is just a fact of life. Your only recourse is to continue creating. Just remember, anyone can knock you off any time, anyone can purchase one of your pieces at a store and send it to China. So don't worry too much about this.

The most dramatic cost savings oversees will be for non-precious metal pieces. In the US, labor costs are so high, it might cost $12 - $18 for a large base metal pendant. In China for example, you might pay $1.50. In Thailand you might pay $5. Thailand and Indonesia are mostly known for their sterling silver work, however. India is good for sterling silver and gold, as well as stone setting. China generally only deals in non-precious metals for the most part. If you're working in sterling silver, and you pay about $12 for quarter size pendants, you might pay about $6-7 in Thailand or Indonesia. Indonesia is more known for their fabrication, while Thailand is more known for their casting.

A couple of tips for going overseas: always insist on a sample, use the most simple and clear English possible in your instructions, and have as many clear pictures and illustrations as possible. Be patient and start with only 1 sample to see how it goes. You don't want to end up with quantities of an entire collection that you hate. If you're sending an original piece, make a photocopy of it and make all your notes on the photocopy. Be prepared to lose your original before they even produce it. It doesn't happen often, but it does happen. It would be great if you can make a second one as a backup. Also, plan that you will definitely be working with a middle man agent. Etsy has agents from overseas that will be able to help you with your castings. This may end up being your best bet because they want to maintain their online reputation, and don't want to be kicked off Etsy.

Assembly

While I'll be discussing in-house assembly, which is my preferred method of assembly, in the next chapter, I wanted to turn briefly to outsourcing assembly. This kind of assembly sounds like a great idea on the surface because you do not have to have as much space in-house for employees, it is something that you probably do not want to deal with yourself, and outsourcing it seemingly leaves you free to work on other things. Also, it can help you avoid various employment-type considerations, such as whether or not to have actual employees, and the legal ramifications of doing so.

However, outsourcing assembly does not work with many business models and jewelry types, as it has many negatives. That is why in my own business I opted for in-house assembly, but have worked hard to make the assembly process as small and easy a job as possible. I have greatly reduced the number of components that I use and I have streamlined the assembly process greatly in order to be able to facilitate an efficient in-house assembly process.

It goes without saying that if you are considering outsourcing your assembly, you need to be selling a lot of the same pieces over and over. Outsourcing assembly is not an economically viable option if your business is mostly made-to-order, or consists of too many small orders of different types of pieces. Whenever you have custom pieces to fill, whether for individuals or stores, you are much better off assembling these custom pieces in-house.

Your options for outsourcing assembling are either: (i) that the factory you are working with for casting or, (ii) you prepare your pieces for assembly at home and then give them to employees who assemble in their own homes. The main problem with getting a factory to either complete or sub-contract your assembly is that they will expect you to source your stones for them and possibly other components. Once you send them stones as an example, it is very difficult for you to keep track of the exact quantity of material sent versus the amount used in your pieces. It is also difficult to make the factories keep track of how many stones were of unusable quality (shape, color, or a small hole for example) and therefore how many went into your actual assembly process. Sourcing your own stones and sending them to a factory could put you in a vulnerable position, exposing yourself to waste and inefficiency. They could also use stones that you would deem unacceptable. You probably know that buying strands of stones that are completely uniform is *very* expensive.

If you do use a factory to assemble your pieces, you want to make sure that all of your components are easy to get on a consistent basis and that they are all of uniform quality, i.e. that you do not have naturally varying ingredients like certain stones or pearls. You cannot assume that the quality of the assembly will be consistently acceptable to you. Factories may do small assembly jobs, such as closing jump rings, in a sub-standard way, leaving you with defective jewelry or having to fix the assembly problems yourself.

To outsource assembly to a person who will do it at home, you will need to have either: (i) a person at your studio carefully preparing kits with all of the materials to be assembled, counting out each component and making sure it is usable, etc., which will cost you a lot of overhead, or (ii) you will have to give the assembly person an overstock of inventory, to account for unusable components or stones and breakage, and again lose control over the use of your inventory and face a loss in efficiency. I have encountered all of these problems in my business and that is why I have decided to assemble my jewelry pieces in-house.

Assembling jewelry in-house is no easy project either, however. Though I think it is a better option than outsourcing assembly, it is important to get the correct systems in place before deciding to assemble in-house, especially if you will delegate much of the assembly process to employees, which I recommend.

Chapter 7

How to Automate Your Business Through Employees

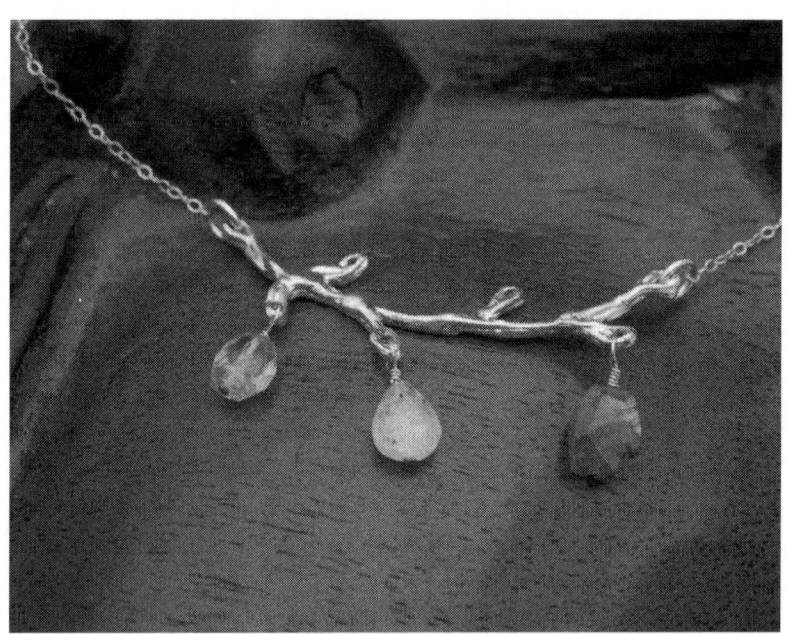

How to Automate Your Business Through Employees

In order for your business to be successful, you need to put efficient systems in place for routine activities such as processing orders and assembling jewelry so that you can spend the majority of your time on creative projects and finding new sources of revenue to grow your business. Your goal with automation through employees should be to be able to walk away from your business for an indefinite period of time and for your employees to be able to fill all of your customer orders without you. This is definitely an achievable goal, if you set up the right infrastructure. This is meant not only to free you up to be able to take a vacation, but also so that you can work day-to-day on growing, and not running, your business. If you do not take the advice in this chapter to heart, you will end up a slave to your business and you will not be able to reap the benefits of having a business that runs itself. The way to create a successful business that you can both walk away from and help grow to new dimensions is to automate the day-to-day activities of the business through employees.

A short note regarding this section: I will be using the word "employees" as a short-hand because it is conventionally understood to mean people that help work on your business. However, I do not mean to say that you should hire employees, as opposed to independent contractors, in a legal sense. Whether or not you choose to hire actual employees (and you should consult other literature or, ideally, an employment lawyer, regarding the difference in the definitions of employees versus independent contractor) should be a decision that you make with all of the legal implications in mind. Once you hire employees you have certain tax and other obligations with respect to them. This book does not discuss these responsibilities, but keep in mind that they exist and that you have to figure out what they are before hiring.

Making your Jewelry

You are going to have a large number of styles in your line or lines and you will want to have a system in place where employees have easy access to directions for assembling each piece of jewelry. When you get an order for several styles, an employee should easily be able to look up the style number of each piece and see what each piece of jewelry looks like, what all of its components are, and how to assemble it. There are many different ways to do this, and you can use one or several of the following suggestions in tandem.

The first idea, which was already mentioned above, is using your website platform to upload pictures of your styles. If you choose this method, each item that you upload will have a style number, which can be part of its sku number, and looking up a piece by style number should bring up a detailed picture, to which you can add (on your own private section of your site), components, and directions for assembly. If you choose this method and create a private section of your website that customers cannot see, then you can feel free to take simple pictures of the jewelry pieces yourself for these purposes. You do not have to have professional pictures for these purposes, but, of course, what you upload to the website for public view should be extremely professional.

Another idea is, as opposed to taking pictures of your jewelry, is to scan the jewelry directly on a photocopier and to write notes on the scanned copy for each piece describing its components and assembly. I also write notes on smaller printouts of my sample board pictures. I take all of these pieces of paper and organize them into a binder, then categorize them in groupings by sample board and finally, create a table of contents that has the style numbers listed in alphabetical order with page number references. If you don't do this, things will get out of hand quickly because your binder will get large and you will not be able to find anything. Each style must be findable instantaneously and easily, or you will run into problems.

In addition to all of this, I maintain an up-to-date spreadsheet that contains the style number, wholesale price, and a short one-line description of every item. This spreadsheet is used for creating invoices, which include the description of the item, which can come straight off of this sheet, but it also comes in handy if someone is having trouble finding an item that they are looking for. This spreadsheet should always be the most up-to-date and it has to be the first place you go when you decide to discontinue or add new items. If you are spinning-off new items off of old styles, you might not take them out of your binders right away, but you have to update the spreadsheet first thing as a matter of course. This spreadsheet will become your best ally.

If your jewelry is at all complicated and it is not obvious how to make it just by looking at a picture, then you will want to create 'recipes' for how to put items together. These are the notes that you should have next to the jewelry pictures for your employees. Recipes basically consist of the components of your jewelry and then any specific assembly instructions. These recipes can be maintained on any of the platforms mentioned above.

The problem with using recipes is that they become outdated very quickly. Despite your best efforts, you will find that you have to change components often because components will go out of stock, or you will find better sources for your components, and you will have to update your recipes to reflect any changes. You will want to also have a master-list of the components you use and where to re-order each one. Also, you will want to be specific in your recipes as to which of your components you are using. As opposed to just writing "jump ring", consider writing which jump ring and from which vendor.

You may find that the recipes are not necessarily used that often because they can be cumbersome. Your employees will often be able to figure out how to make the jewelry just by seeing a picture, without looking at a recipe. But you will still need, for the most-part, to have these recipes in place as backup in case any questions arise or if your jewelry is not completely obvious to make. It is for this reason that I try to streamline my designs as much as possible and make it as easy as possible for employees to put things together quickly and intuitively. You should not be discouraged from making the art that you want to make, just realize that if your jewelry is complicated in any way you will have to maintain constantly updated documents.

When you are first starting out in your jewelry business, you tend to have tons of different components because you have a variety of different inspirations and have not yet learned to edit. The best thing you can do for yourself as you progress into a larger business is to greatly edit the number of components you have, find components that you can source affordably and consistently that will work on many pieces, and try to have as few components as you can in each style. This is important for three reasons: (i) it will streamline your assembly process greatly and make assembly much easier for your employees; (ii) it will allow you to negotiate much better pricing on your components if you are buying them in larger quantities, therefore increasing your margins; and (iii) it will avoid you being left with small quantities of lots of different components, of which you do not have enough to re-use for new styles.

Other Ways to Automate

There are things other than jewelry-making that can be automated through instructions. All of the things that you do in your business change on a regular basis, so you either want to update your instructions on a regular basis, like the recipes, or you need to make sure that the tasks that you automate are so simple that anybody can do them.

Here is a list of items you should try to automate through your employees:

- Processing credit cards;
- Branding and packaging the jewelry;
- Shipping the jewelry;
- Organizing inventory (Note: the best jewelry inventory software I know of is Craft Maker Pro);
- Re-ordering jewelry components and other supplies;
- Processing online orders;
- Interfacing with customers;
- Creating sample boards;
- Accounts receivables (tracking unpaid orders);
- Tracking back-orders (pieces that were ordered by customers when you were out of stock- remembering to order the pieces and send them out when they arrive); and
- Creating invoices.

Chapter 8

Getting Your Line into Stores on Your Own

In general, you do not want to spend your time doing sales and getting your line into stores. This can largely be delegated to reps, which you will want to get as soon as possible. However, in order to get a rep, you generally need to show them that you are already sold in several stores and it also lends you credibility on your website to be able to name the stores you are in. So you will have to get yourself into at least 5 - 10 stores on your own before you can largely delegate this sales function. This advice should not stop you from approaching reps as soon as possible, but you should know that it may be hard to get them to represent your line before you can show them where you are carried

Types of Stores to Target
i. Consignment Stores

The first selling issue you will want to consider is leaving your jewelry on consignment versus making outright sales. It is clearly better to get outright sales that are paid for. You will want to try and limit the number of consignment stores that you are in because this uses up your inventory on pieces that you have not been paid for, costs you a lot in overhead, and increases the risk you bear for pieces getting lost or stolen. Therefore, try as much as you can to get stores to buy your jewelry outright.

When stores ask for consignment, you can generally say that you don't do it. But, if you are having trouble getting your foot in the door with the first couple of stores, you can opt for consignment in order to build your credibility and you do not have to disclose your consignment arrangement with other stores. The other advantage to consignment is that if you have your jewelry on consignment in a busy store that does a lot of business, you can actually do more business with that store than any other non-consignment account. This is because when stores buy from you outright, they generally purchase anywhere from 1-3 times per year, and each time they order about 10-50 pieces, with about 30 pieces being an average number. However, when you leave your jewelry on consignment, assuming that the store likes your product, you can generally leave a lot of items and they will make efforts to move the product. They will also generally take discontinued items as well as new, untested ones, making them a great place to try out new styles.

You should note that the more products you have in a store, and the greater presence you have there, the more likely you are to sell. The very first store I was in was actually on a consignment basis. The store was owned by my 'customer mentor'. It was a very busy store in the heart of downtown San Diego and, although I dealt with that store on consignment, I was grossing about $1000 per month for several years, until the store closed.

ii. Co-ops/Incubators

Another type of arrangement to generally avoid in the long-term, but which is also a good way to get your foot in the door, is a co-op or incubator where you have to rent a space in a store in order to sell your jewelry. You generally want to avoid having to pay any store for space because any situation where you have to spend money to make money is less than optimal. However, these co-ops and incubators can be a good place to start and helps your brand build credibility. You should know that, in general, co-op and consignment stores are not responsible for customer theft or even for their own employees ringing your merchandise up wrong, so this is an extra negative when considering arrangements other than outright sales.

The plus to consignment and co-ops is that, if inventory is not an issue for you, it is basically equivalent to selling at markets, except that you are in essence paying someone else to do the selling for you. Anyone who has spent long days at markets selling their own jewelry will know this to be a benefit. While these are not as good as outright sales, they may be a good transitional step.

iii. Apparel Stores/ Gift Shops/ Galleries vs. Specialty Jewelry Stores

In terms of what stores to actively target for outright sales, different jewelry lines do better in different types of stores, for different reasons. Apparel stores are great for selling less expensive, impulse type jewelry that improves an outfit. Very unique-looking jewelry often does well at gift shops or galleries. Also, many galleries prefer local artists, so these are a good type of store to target in your geographic home turf. It can be more difficult to generate high sales at exclusively-jewelry stores because you are competing with so many other jewelry brands, so these are not necessarily the first stores to target, but feel free to try some of those as well.

iv. Department Stores

It is natural for beginning jewelry designers to dream of getting into large department stores. They can be, of course, lucrative and prestigious to be in if you can break in, but it is notoriously hard to do so. Therefore, while most beginning designers think that they should concentrate on sending samples to and trying to meet buyers from the biggest department stores, you should know that, unless you have unlimited capacity for producing inventory and large means, it does not make sense to concentrate on department stores at first.

I have been watching jewelry lines in department stores for several years and it is amazing to me how few lines actually manage to stand the test of time and get carried by department stores on an ongoing basis. I therefore do not recommend the department store route for any business without large means and production capability. If you are still interested in department stores for the prestige or large potential market share, I highly recommend that you grow into that business model organically by building your business through lots of smaller accounts first.

In order to get into department stores, you need to either: (i) have great connections, (ii) be picked out by one of their buyers at one of the exclusive tradeshows that they attend, which cost a lot of money to get into and is a long shot, (iii) send your samples to their headquarters and be aware that this is pretty much where samples go to die, (iv) contact their fashion directors, which are founds on lists for purchase on Infomat or Fashion Index, (v) impress a jewelry sales person, who can put you in touch with the department manager, or can put you in touch with buyers.

You can make plenty of money and build up an extremely viable business from stores other than major department stores, so my recommendation is that you spend your time elsewhere unless you have a concrete reason to believe that you have an in. However, there is one other way to get into department stores if you have your heart set on it: you can hire a very expensive rep or agency through a head hunter that has relationships with department stores. This is not my method because these reps are costly and hard to come by. While I discuss traditional rep relationships in the next chapter, if you think it is the right thing for your business, you can also consider these specialized reps a possibility.

Be aware that buyers for department stores require you to already have the infrastructure in place to be able to fill large orders on demand. This causes sort of a chicken-and-egg problem for small designers because most small designers do not have the funds to fill department store-size orders before having the capital

Getting Your Line into Stores on Your Own

from the department stores to invest towards production. (Unless you chose to go for outside investments). You therefore have to already be in enough other stores to have grown your business sufficiently before approaching department stores or have basically unlimited funds and production capabilities.

If you are lucky enough to get picked up by a department store, they usually try your line in one store first. Often times they will offer you the opportunity to do a trunk show in the store, which is a temporary setup where you are present and interact with customers. Based on sales from that 1-3 day event, you may get picked up for one store. If you do well in one store, they may expand their orders to more stores in the region. That jump alone will wreak havoc on any small jewelry operation. You will have to shell out a lot of money and effort in order to fill orders for several large stores. Plus, department stores are notorious for: (i) making you take back merchandise that does not sell, which is a shock to any small business' finances, (ii) if you do not meet their projected sales from one year to the next, they expect you to share financially in the 'loss' of sales, as compared to projections, if you want to continue to be carried in their stores, or (iii) deduct large sums of money otherwise owed to you for shipping, trade discounts, charge-backs, and markdown allowances. It is essential, for all of the reasons mentioned above, to make sure that your business is not reliant on just one account for its survival and you don't want to have more than 15% of your business reliant on department stores, in the aggregate. Department stores can drop your line unexpectedly overnight and offer draconian terms. You have to diversify.

v. Online Stores

There are several online stores that sell many different designers and appeal to different types of markets, from high-end stores to edgy ones to overstock and mark-down ones, etc. You may have to try several different online shops to find a forum where your brand sells well. Some shops buy outright from you and others will do drop shipping, where you keep your own inventory, they notify you when you have an order, and you ship it. They keep a commission on the sale for what is essentially a referral service, since they do not buy or house your jewelry. Some stores will require online exclusivity and I do not recommend granting that unless the store is willing to buy significant amounts from you outright and will promote you.

Some examples of online stores that I recommend checking out are www.activeendeavors.com and www.shopbop.com. There is an additional category of online stores that are not selective, where you can upload anything you want. Examples of these are www.etsy.com and www.amazon.com. There are also shopping search engines like www.thefind.com or www.googleshopping.com that you can contact. You generally have to fill out an application to get accepted onto their network and then upload products through a feed, normally an Excel spreadsheet. The purpose of these shopping search engines is to link consumer traffic back to your website for a small percentage of sales. There are also online discounters like www.Zulily.com and www.Groupon.com. All of these options are viable and you will want to try out as many of them as you can because no one source is likely to produce a huge number of sales right away.

How to Approach Stores

As you are starting to discover stores that you would like be in, it is helpful to go into the stores, start browsing, and strike up a friendly conversation with the person working there. Try to get a feel of who this person is and whether they are an employee or an owner. Introduce yourself and say that you have your own jewelry line that you think would make a great addition to the store. You should always be wearing your own jewelry when you go into stores trying to make connections, as this will be an obvious conversation-starter and way to describe your line. Ask the representative you are talking to who the store's buyer is and try to get them to tell you when the buyer will be there.

When you are in a mode of trying to get into stores, you should try to always be carrying about 3-4 sample pieces, in addition to what you are wearing, in a little box with compartments, as well as a look-book or some printed photos,. You should have these materials with you, even if you are planning to come back for an actual appointment with the buyer, because whoever you are talking to (and ideally hitting it off with!) might ask you to see a few things on the spot. You never want to be in a situation where you have to say you will come back and miss the opportunity to show your merchandise in person. Being prepared at all times maximizes your chances of making sales and getting a buyer appointment.

Use the information that you get from the person and try and come back when you understand that a buyer will be there, even if you do not have an official appointment. When you show up to a store with the expectation that a buyer will be there, you should ideally bring all of your samples with you. It may be inconvenient to drag them around and your first time meeting a buyer will probably not be an official appointment to go through your samples, but you never know when a buyer is going to have the time, as well as be in the mood to browse through your selection, and it is optimal if that is always an option on the spot.

Do not bother making cold calls or sending emails to new stores. This approach will simply not work and will basically use up whatever introductory goodwill you might have when introducing yourself in person. Since it is very unlikely that anyone will respond to you, don't bug the stores with cold contact only then to walk in with the knowledge that they have already snubbed you. Instead, always go in directly and in person. This approach takes more time, of course, and you may think that you will save time in the long-run by at least calling. However, from personal experience, I know that this does not, and will not, work.

There is no substitute to making the time to go out to the stores in person, or sending a rep, but someone has to go.

What you will find is that the average store buyer is an extremely elusive individual. They are generally never there, extremely busy, or obviously avoiding you like the plague. For this reason, I have discovered that my biggest tip is to have your samples, either the entire set or a selection of your best work, with you and to leave these samples and print materials, both with contact information, with the employee that you talked to. You can tell the employee at the store that you fully trust them with the samples and that the store's buyer can feel free to look at your samples at their convenience. This will greatly increase your chances of your jewelry being seen. Though this may seem like a risky and unconventional thing to do, when entrusted with precious samples, people are usually inclined to keep them safe and to actually look through them without being put on the spot. They do not automatically feel like they owe you if you do not leave something behind. This technique has gotten me into some very exclusive stores and, of course, I have always been able to get my samples back safe and sound.

Territories

Be aware when you are trying to get into stores, many will expect to be the exclusive vendor of your product within a certain radius, if it's a busy area, perhaps the block, or perhaps an entire small town. Therefore, you should think about which stores you would most like to get into before approaching them and try to approach them in your order of preference (highest to lowest). Of course, it may not ultimately be your choice what stores accept your line, but you should try and prioritize appointments to the extent you can so that you can avoid getting shut out of stores you would have preferred to be in had you approached them first.

This expectation of exclusivity within a certain geographic area will also apply to your reps. If you are already in a particular store to which you granted certain exclusivity, your reps will not be able to get you into neighboring stores. Whenever you can avoid granting exclusivity or minimizing it as much as you can, you should seek to do so. But, since you do not know what terms you will be able to negotiate before you walk in the door, try to make it a habit to scan the area before approaching any store and prioritize.

Conflicts of Interest

If you are starting your jewelry line selling at markets and craft fairs,(which I did for several years when I started my business, you will probably have to choose between doing that and being carried in stores. This is because stores will not want to see you selling your product for cheaper than they carry it elsewhere. Usually if you don't charge the full store retail price at a market, which is very hard to do in a market setting, stores will not carry your items, knowing that the same pieces are available in the region at a cheaper price.

There are two ways around this conflict. The first is trying to get into stores that are not in the same geographic region in your usual sale markets. They may not mind if you sell at a market in San Diego, for instance, if they are a store in Minnesota. The second is to have different lines. Of course, this is not necessarily for the beginning jewelry designer, but if you can assure the stores that you have one more exclusive line for stores and another line of completely different pieces that will be available only in markets, this should not pose a conflict. You can therefore look at markets as a viable way to sell designs that you made but are determined you are not going to market and sell as part of your cohesive collection when you were editing down.

Remember that I warned that most stores do not like it if you sell your pieces directly on your website. This is because they do not want customers to be able to just come into their stores to look at pieces, try them on, go home, and order them online. However, they are not usually explicit about this prohibition. They may frown upon it but, ultimately, no particular store will be paying your bills on its own and the amount of money you can potentially make off of your website some day is greater than what you could make from any particular store. My advice is to sell online when you are mature enough to do so.

Secrets of a Successful Jewelry Brand

Chapter 9

"Reps"

What You Should Expect from Your Rep

A rep is an independent sales representative who represents multiple lines and is paid on commission from generating orders for your line. Reps usually represent a particular territory, which can be part of a state, a whole state, or a region encompassing multiple states. You usually cannot have more than one rep within their specifically defined territory, but you can get reps in various areas. The more reps you have and the more territories you are in, the higher the cost, both money-wise and time-wise. You have to send each rep new sample boards each time you update the line, as well as recall discontinued items from all of them. The time and inventory to accomplish this really adds up. The greatest number of territories that I have ever been represented in at one time is eight.

Reps can sell your merchandise through several different methods. One way is to be a 'road rep', meaning that they are on the go, physically driving from store to store to manage existing accounts, attend appointments, and try to get lines into new stores. Another way is to be a 'tradeshow rep' (in addition to being a road rep), where they represent several lines at once at a number of tradeshows. Keep in mind that with a tradeshow rep, you are expected to pay not only a regular sales commission, but also the costs of entering the tradeshow. A third way reps can sell your line is to either own or belong to a showroom, where they also show

113

many different lines. Like with tradeshows, if you want your line to be featured in a showroom, there is a monthly fee that you have to pay in addition to regular commissions on sales. Lastly, a rep will use your resources - look-book, line sheets, and website - to generate orders. They will expect a commission for any method through which they generate sales, even if they only refer customers and do not work solely through appointments. They will also expect commissions for re-orders from customers that they generated for as long as you are working with them. Other than fees charged at showrooms or tradeshows, a standard commission is, on average, 15% of the gross wholesale price of any piece sold. Some reps will try to negotiate a commission of up to 20%, but you can usually push back and say that you offer only 15%. Some reps will insist on 20% because they are in a sparse territory and have to drive long distances and put in a lot of hours to generate sales, which can be the case, so they will stand their ground. But, usually if you push back to 15%, most reps will accept this as a standard commission.

Some reps also work with sub-reps. Sub-reps are road reps who are affiliated with a particular rep or rep group who has generated a network. Most often, you will negotiate directly with the main rep with the network and you should still expect to pay the 15% commission, with them working out their own commission structure with their sub-reps. However, sometimes you can negotiate with the sub-reps directly. These are often inexperienced reps that do not yet have clients and you can sometimes negotiate a 10% commission from them because they are new, trying to build a client base, and reputability in order to become independent. These can be desirable situations economically because of the lower commission, but, in general, you will want to find yourself established reps so as to get your product into stores quickly without wasting time.

When you start doing business with a rep, they will occasionally ask you to send them, in addition to sample boards, free samples of jewelry that they can wear to appointments. Having your reps wear your jewelry does, in fact, help business so you should accommodate this request and accept it as a cost of doing business, knowing that you will probably never see that jewelry again. If reps want to buy additional jewelry from you directly, they usually expect to get it at wholesale price minus their commission (so about 85% of wholesale). This is also standard and should be generally accommodated without argument.

Here's an important pro-tip: I highly recommend that as you're starting to work with more and more stores through reps, you keep a file on each store with as much information as you can gather on them, including name of buyer, name of owner, name of employees, phone numbers, and most importantly e-mails. Relationships with reps don't last forever and once you're no longer working with the rep, these files will come in very handy. If you don't have these important names and emails, you will be nothing but a telemarketer when you attempt to call in the future. Learn from my mistakes. I did not do this often and ended up leaving a lot of business on the table.

Finding Reps

The number one question I get asked by other jewelry designers is how to find reps. There is no easy answer to this and it is, honestly, one of the hardest parts of the business. There is no easy go-to directory of jewelry reps, except for Accessories the Magazine - www.accessoriesmagazine.com. I am currently working on compiling a directory of reps together, so email me at info@YourOwnJewelryLine.com if you'd like to know more. Here are all the 'hard' ways to go about finding reps, which is what I have done and continue to do.

i. Asking Stores

Most stores get their merchandise either through reps, through going to shows, or a combination of both. Therefore, asking stores that you are either carried in or interested in can be a good resource. The best technique for this is to start locally and work your way out geographically. You can certainly expand though if you have reason to believe that your jewelry will sell well in a particular region. I got feedback that my style of jewelry would sell well in the Northwest. I therefore got myself a plane ticket to Portland, Oregon and literally walked from store to store in the areas I wanted to be in. Using a little gumption, I found my rep in the Northwest on that trip.

Whenever you go to stores looking for reps, remember that you should always carry a few samples with you, as when you are visiting stores to make sales. Often, when I engage in this activity, stores that like my line set me up with their rep and also proceed to make their first order on the basis of the samples and print materials I've brought. You never know whether a certain visit will result in a sale or a rep, so don't come empty-handed!

Do not be surprised that many stores do not work with reps and therefore will not be able to give you any contacts. The farther stores are away from cities with major jewelry shows - which are New York, Los Angeles, Atlanta, Las Vegas, northern California, and the Seattle-area - the more likely that the stores will be working with reps and be good resources for you.

ii. Searching Jewelry Sites Online

I also search other jewelry brand sites online. I am familiar with hundreds of jewelry lines that I consider to be my peers and I go onto each of their websites to look for reps. Only about 1 out of 50 websites will list the rep, so this method is extremely time consuming, but it will allow you to start building a small contact base and build out your network.

iii. Online Links to Previously-Found Reps

My next method is Googling reps I discovered from the first two methods to ferret out others. Their names will often appear next to other reps in various lists, on websites, show directories, events, etc., which can also generate leads. Any new reps found through this method can, in turn, of course, also be Googled to further expand your network. Eventually you start seeing that some names pop up most often on your searches and you are therefore able to ascertain who the big reps are for the major lines in the regions that you are interested.

iv. Tradeshows and Show Rooms

You can also find reps at tradeshows and show rooms. Tradeshows publish directories of each entrant at the tradeshow that has a booth. Most people who have booths are independent jewelry designers, so this is not always helpful for finding reps. However, if you see a name on the directory associated with several lines, you can bet that that person is a rep. You can also walk through tradeshows and show rooms to meet reps, but they will not be willing to talk to you during the shows. Since they will be on duty trying to sell their other lines, the most you can hope for is to introduce yourself and pick up a business card for further follow-up. Do not try and get into a detailed discussion about your line during shows where reps are representing other lines.

v. Accessories Magazine

In addition, Accessories Magazine publishes a list of reps and showrooms close to tradeshow season. Not all of the issues have this, it cannot be found online, and it is a bit expensive to buy. But if you can locate the issues with this directory during tradeshow season, it can be very helpful.

vi. Recommendations from Other Reps

Once you do find some reps, you can ask them to recommend other reps, because by virtue of their line of work they tend to be very well-connected people. Of course, you should not insinuate that you want any information on reps within their territories, but if you are looking to expand they can often be helpful in hooking you up with colleagues in other areas.

vii. Helping Reps Find You

The last way you find reps is actually for reps to find you. In my case, I found my very first rep in this way. After I was carried in a few stores locally in San Diego I had gotten into myself, covering San Diego's main territories,, my sister Noa Tal (who is ghost-writing this book) offered to take my line to northern California and show it to stores. One of the stores that placed an order with her happened to be unwrapping my jewelry package when a rep walked into the store. The rep immediately fell in love with the line and actually asked the store owner how to get in touch with me. I have worked with many reps over the years, and they tend to come and go, but this one has stayed with me pretty much since the beginning. This method cannot be relied on, but it is great when it happens!

What to Do When you Find a Rep

Once you have a rep's contact info, you have to sell yourself. Ideally, by the time you approach one, you will already be in at least 5-10 stores. You should definitely mention this and discuss your track record on sales. Also have your look-book handy share and any other professional materials you would want them to use when making sales. If you are further along with your line, a rep might agree to take you on just by viewing your website online. But, if you are having trouble convincing one, you should ask them for permission to send samples.

The dynamic with reps can be tricky. When you are first starting out, you will feel like you are on a job interview, where they are interviewing you. The reality, of course, is that you are hiring them. But they will not want to waste their time on a line that they do not think will be worth their while. Until you have a proven track record, you are the one on trial, so to speak. As you grow your business, the leverage shifts and you can get a number of reps to represent you. They, in turn, will be trying to sell you on their skills. If you really have no track record, you should just do your best to impress them with pictures, samples, your story, and anything else you have to show. However, if you are already in a significant number of stores and can prove that you have been doing decently well, you might as well consider yourself to be the interviewer. Confidence goes a long way, in this or any business.

When approaching a rep, think of your business as a successful one that reps would feel lucky to represent and try to interview them in the way that a real employer would interview an employee. One way to accomplish this is, if there is a rep in another territory that you want to interview and you have the means to do it, you can fly them out to meet with you. This will immediately put you in control of the situation, put you in the driver's seat as the interviewer, and show the rep that you are serious. I do not recommend doing this with every rep, but if there is one that you feel would really be worth your while, it is a good idea.

Lastly, you should know that it is worth pursuing potentially good reps, even if they do not agree to represent you the first time. It could be that your line is not yet mature enough, or that you are not in enough stores. But, it also could be that they do not feel that your line is synergistic with the other lines they happen to be representing at the time. Reps want to take on lines that will go together well with lines that they are currently representing, but will not necessarily be in direct competition with them.

With my line, I had a great rep that I knew I wanted, but when I first approached her, she said that my line was not a good fit for because it was too similar to another line she was already representing. I kept in touch with her and, two years later, I showed her my new collection. She agreed to represent me and she has turned out to be one of my best reps, getting me lots of business. Do not give up if you are told no the first time. Keep all of your contacts organized, available to you, and continue to check in periodically. You never know when something will work out.

Things to Discuss When Interviewing a Rep

There are several things you should consider discussing with your rep when you set up an interview. It might seem natural to ask ideally, how much business they can bring you. In my experience, there *is no relationship* between the kind of business a rep promises to bring and the amount of business they actually generate. In fact, I have found that the more business a rep promises to bring, usually the less they actually do. Therefore, feel free to ask this question but always take the answer with a grain of salt.

Reps are very busy and they represent many lines in the stores and accounts that they interact with. They are also always on the road and driving so, understandably, they are not always the best at getting back to you. But, because you sometimes do need to speak to them to relay information, discontinue an item, etc., I recommend that you set an expectation from the beginning, in your first interview, that, while you do not intend to bother them for no reason, you do intend to hear back from them within a reasonable period of time when you initiate contact. If a rep does not seem cooperative about this point, they will probably not be receptive when you actually do try to talk, making this is an important point to iron out. Pro tip: if a rep goes AWOL, chances are they are not making enough money off your line, it is now more of a burden than an asset, and they are avoiding the issue all together. It's time to reconsider the relationship and consider pulling your line back.

"Reps"

A rep relationship will last from 6 months to years, with an average of about 2 years, which is all normal.

Chapter 10

What to Expect at Tradeshows

What to Expect at Tradeshows

What is a Tradeshow?

Usually held in a large convention center, a Tradeshow is open to individuals in a certain industry and encompasses hundreds of different booths with sellers trying to find buyers for their goods. Tradeshows usually last about 3 days. There are jewelry-specific tradeshows, accessory tradeshows, apparel tradeshows, and gift tradeshows, all of which a jewelry line can be a part of. Many shows are organized by ENK, www.enkshows.com, hosting shows around the country, the big ones for jewelry being Accessorie Circuit, Coterie, and ENKVEGAS. Two other big show organizers are MAGIC in Las Vegas - www.magiconline.com, and the show at the Wynn hotel. In New York, the JA show, www.JA-newyork.com, is known for more 'blingy' jewelry. The Gift and Apparel shows in Atlanta, www.americasmart.com, are the biggest for that part of the country. Other major shows include:

- The California Gift shows - www.californiamarketcenter.com and www.LAmart.com
- The Dallas Apparel & Accessories Show - www.dallasmarketcenter.com
- NY NOW www.NYnow.com
- NW Market show in Tigard Oregon www.northwestmarket.org
- Trend Seattle Show www.trendsnw.com

125

- Seattle Gift show www.seattlegiftshow.com
- The San Mateo Gift and Apparel shows - www.sanmateoexpo.org
- The San Francisco International Gift Fair www.sfigf.com
- The Denver Gift and Apparel, Jewelry and Resort show, WESA (Western show), Apparel Show www.denvermart.com

There are three ways to be part of a tradeshow: buying your own booth, being represented by a rep that routinely goes to tradeshows as one of their lines, and finding another artisan or jewelry maker that will split a booth with you. If you exhibit in a showroom that is in the same building as one of the marts, then the showroom will get traffic during the show as well.

An ENK Accessories Trade Show
From www.enkshows.com

What to Expect at Tradeshows

Having Your Own Booth

In order to have your own booth at a tradeshow, you need to get accepted. It goes without saying that some tradeshows are pickier than others. Buying your own booth at a tradeshow ranges anywhere from $3,000-$10,000, depending on which show you are applying to and what type of spot you want.

In addition to the cost of the booth, any display at a tradeshow has to be top-notch. You cannot come to a tradeshow with a display like you would have at a craft fair, like folding tables or non-matching displays. You have to have professional, cohesive shelving and displays, a large, beautiful sign, laminated, high-quality photos of your work to attract buyers into your booth, and you have to spend money on incidentals, like extra lighting and help. Baroni Designs - www.baronidesigns.com - has a nice picture of their booth on the website. This is one of the lower cost, but still nice, setups I have seen. The ENK website has a great short video showing the vibe of a tradeshow (Circuit) and it gives you some great snippets of various jewelry booths, you can get an idea of what kind of booths are out there www.enkshows.com/circuit/#video . Available storage for all of your tradeshow equipment in between shows is also a necessity. You will need access to a large vehicle to transport all of this equipment to and from tradeshows. Though you can spend thousands of dollars on a good setup for tradeshows, it is only worth it if you are planning to attend tradeshows on a regular basis.

It makes no sense to invest in this kind of professional setup for one show.

Aside from the cost of the booth, all of the displays, and materials you will bring, you have to spend a significant amount of time considering the layout of your booth. You will want to make sure that you do not create a trapping, insular space where people feel like they have to walk into the booth in order to see anything and will get trapped in a conversation with you. The booth should feel open and inviting, but you should have a significant amount of jewelry visible on display for people walking by.

You also want to make sure that you exude positive, confident energy. In an ideal world, you want buyers to walk by and see you engaged in conversation with other buyers, taking orders. Buyers should feel as if you are doing a lot of business, like they are free to look around your booth without any pressure, and they have to wait a few minutes to approach you. Of course, it is not easy to summon buyers out of thin air. Therefore, it is a good idea to recruit a few friends to come with you to your first couple of trade shows and to have them check in periodically to make sure you appear to be in conversation a significant amount of the time. You may want to have a stack of order forms that you can pretend to be reviewing and editing in order to look busy when you're by yourself in the booth. If you have to prepare some fake ones so your order forms are not blank, so be it.

There is nothing more off-putting to a buyer than to see a morose, melancholy seller sitting alone in a booth. This morose-

What to Expect at Tradeshows

looking person is very likely to be you if you don't take steps to counteract it. With everything you will have spent on the tradeshow, between the admission and the setup, when a few hours go by, then a few more, and you have not made enough to recoup your costs, let alone made any profit, you are likely to sink into a sort of funk and exude desperation. There is no surer bet than this to send all of your potential buyers flying to other booths. Bring a friend or friends and make sure you are able to be dynamic, positive, and approachable, but a little careless. If you do not think that you can control your emotions well enough to exude this positive energy, no matter what your sales and no matter what the outcome, do not represent yourself at a trade show. Hire a rep to do it - they are trained professionals who play exactly this game.

In addition to recruiting friends and by-standers to come by so you don't appear alone, you really want to make sure that you have actual customers coming by for sales purposes. You should be sending elites, postcards, and personally calling all of your customers and potential customers to let them know about the trade show and you should be making appointments with as many of them as you can at the tradeshow. The bulk of the people that will be visiting your booth will actually be people that you invite, so you have to make sure to send out these invitations and get plenty of appointments booked. Do not expect lots of random buyers who do not have an association with you to stop by your booth for more than a minute.

At the show, you should try and collect business cards from everyone who stops by your booth, but you should only do this with people who have already spent 30-60 seconds in your booth. The goal is to collect the business cards, but not if asking for them scares people away. You therefore want to make sure that you are only asking people who are showing some kind of interest and are not likely to bolt the second you approach them.

You should also prepare a little postcard to give each visitor that contains a representative photo or collage, your brand name and booth number so that they can come back or follow up later. This could be the same postcard mailer that you send invitees. Cards like this are especially important at trade shows because most buyers check out each booth for a second to scope out where they'll return to before actually spending any time there. They can easily forget to come back to you without a handy reminder.

Do not be surprised if you spend thousands of dollars on a tradeshow and do not do well your first time around. There is a well-known paradox in the jewelry business which is that, on the one hand, buyers are looking for new and exciting merchandise but, on the other hand, they want to buy from proven lines. They will often not buy from a line that they see at a tradeshow the first time. Many buyers will wait to see you around at a second or third show to make sure your line is selling and has stood the test of time before buying themselves.

What to Expect at Tradeshows

Before you decide to spend money on a tradeshow, you should try to go and see one first. You should be familiar with the kinds of lines carried at the show and what the booth setups are like before you determine if it is right for you. Trade shows can be quite strict when it comes to allowing people in the door. They really want serious buyers and they do not want random lookers-on or designers showing up trying to poach ideas without the intention of buying.

Tradeshows usually demand to see several proofs that you are in the business. Many list their exact requirements on their website, so check before you make a commitment. One form of proof is a business card with the physical location of a store, which you probably will not have. Yet, another form of proof can be a website. They do allow online retailers to enter so if you have a website, they usually will not inspect whether you sell only your own products or also other peoples'. Lastly, they usually want to see purchase orders evidencing purchases you have made. You can bring along and show them purchase orders for components and materials from manufacturers, and that will usually do the trick. The last way would be if you know someone who is selling at the tradeshow or working in a booth, and then you can come in as a guest.

Being Represented by a Rep at a Tradeshow

What I have discussed so far regarding having your own booth at a trade show is for established lines, because you need to have the money to pay the entrance fee, all of the costs of display, and enough variety of available styles to bring and still be organized in its presentation. For most beginning jewelry designers, I do not recommend setting up your own booth at a trade show. However, you can still get into one by being represented by a rep that routinely does trade shows or have your line sold in a showroom.

A rep who goes to a tradeshow rents a large booth and velcros your sample boards to the wall, along with all of the other lines they are representing. You therefore need to create professional sample boards in advance of a tradeshow. (Head back to Chapter 4 for the how-to.) Know that a rep will expect you to have pre-made, ready sample boards that are all the same kind for a trade show so that they can be displayed side by side.

If you don't want your setup to be just your sample boards velcroed to the wall, you have to negotiate a special display. With these displays, you usually have to show up at the tradeshow and set it up yourself. If you removed any jewelry from sample boards to create alternative displays, you will also have to be dismantling these displays and re-creating your sample boards on your own. Be prepared that not all spots in a rep's booth are created equal and when you are starting out in trade shows you will probably find that your line does not have the best spot in the booth.

The fee for being represented by a rep at the tradeshow is generally between $150 - $500, depending on which tradeshow and which spot you will get within the rep's booth. It is possible to

What to Expect at Tradeshows

negotiate with the rep that instead of this fee you will pay an increased commission on sales, for example 20% instead of 15% of sales at the tradeshow.

You may wonder how many orders you should expect from a tradeshow in order to determine whether or not it will be worth it for you. This is very hard to predict, as they can really range from 0 to 20 orders of anywhere from $100 - $1,000 each, but you should generally not expect very many. For me, I have one successful tradeshow that gets me a lot of orders, but generally I do not find them to be a good use of my money and time.

When you first start your relationship with a rep that does tradeshows in addition to regular store sales, they usually expect you to allow them to represent your line in the show they do and to pay them a fee, plus commission. I do recommend that you do at least the first show with them to show your support and see if the experience works for you. But, if you find that you do not generate good sales and is not financially viable for your business, you can feel free to tell the reps that you will not participate in any more shows and that you just want them doing normal commission sales.

You should also know that reps will generally not want you to be anywhere near their booth during a tradeshow, unless you are specifically setting up or dismantling your displays. Often, you won't not even be in the same city as the tradeshow when it is taking place. Do not try to show up in person to hang around the booth and see how sales are going – reps *hate* that.

I generally find that the quality, in terms of repeat orders, of the customers at tradeshows is not as high as accounts that reps regularly open up on the road for two reasons. The first is that, in tradeshows, customers come from all over the country and are therefore not likely to reorder and be repeat customers since your rep will not see them again until the next show. The second is that, , if the customers demand unfavorable terms, such as paying in the future, and then they do not remit payment, the reps have less leverage to force them to pay because they are less likely to have a relationship with those customers.

There are whole tradeshows or parts of tradeshows where, rather than placing orders for jewelry, buyers come and purchase jewelry outright. This method of sales is called 'cash and carry' and it is not common for major designers to participate in these sorts of shows. Cash and carry tends to be for less expensive jewelry that is not usually hand-crafted, because designers need an enormous amount of inventory at the show in order to participate. It will probably not be right for you if you do more expensive or custom jewelry. I mention it here though because the cash and carry section of a tradeshow often looks like the busiest section and you may be wondering why you are not doing as much business. Just keep in mind that, if you are creating your own jewelry, this is probably not the section for you. If you are an importer, rather than a designer, or your goal is to move large quantities of simple designs, like hoop earrings, then you may very well consider cash and carry.

Lastly, if your line is in a showroom, depending on the location of the showroom, your line may also be represented at the tradeshow. If the showroom is in the same building as the show, then buyers will also walk through the showroom while attending, and there will be no extra costs to participate. This is a positive consideration for being in a showroom that sits adjacent to a tradeshow. But, if your showroom is not directly adjacent to the tradeshow, the showroom will likely rent a booth inside, and expect all of the lines in the showroom to participate in the cost, which is generally steep.

Overall, I do not usually recommend tradeshows for beginning designers until they have a line of a certain size because of the high costs involved and the generally meager sales one can expect. Huge, established lines will rent booths at shows, but even they are usually sitting empty, trying to look busy, and there are surprisingly few buyers that come out to most tradeshows in person. Unless you have excess capital and an already established line, tradeshows are just not a good use of your resources.

Showrooms

Showrooms are owned by reps, or groups of reps, where buyers will go to purchase goods at pretty much any time. They are permanent fixtures and are usually clustered in the same building. Sometimes, showrooms will be adjacent to tradeshows that are going on and they will do more business when there is a tradeshow, but they operate year-round. A showroom will have dozens of lines and they can be all jewelry, or jewelry can be mixed with apparel or other gift items.

Showrooms charge rent to the lines that are represented there. You can expect to pay anywhere from $200 - $500 a month just for your line to be exhibited, depending on which room and which spot your line will have. This is in addition to commission on goods sold, which usually runs about 15%, like with normal rep sales. In addition, showrooms that are not in the same building as the tradeshow expect all of their lines to participate handsomely in any tradeshows that the showroom participates in, which can add up to extra costs, as I discussed in the section on tradeshows. If you are interested in having your line in a showroom, you can go check one out any time. The showroom venues are often located in the various Mart buildings and each city usually has a list of venues. Accessories Magazine also lists showrooms. You can show up at showrooms in person and speak to whoever is working there to get informational particulars on any room you like.

Depending on where a particular showroom is located, during local tradeshows, they will either exhibit your lines in their rooms adjacent to the tradeshows, or the showroom will rent a booth at the tradeshow. If you visit showrooms at any time of the year when there is no tradeshow in town, do not be surprised to find that there is almost nobody there. As far as I am concerned, the only lines that should be represented in showrooms are very large, established lines that get large amounts of unsolicited repeat business year-round. For the average starting designer, a showroom is not usually a worthwhile investment, despite what the showroom owner will tell you, because of the fixed monthly cost to be there, often resulting in no sales.

Chapter 11

Account Management

Account Management

Receiving Orders

Orders for jewelry will usually come to you through reps, if you're using them, and the orders usually come in through fax. Do not bother trying to get reps to use other more contemporary methods, such as email. They are very fixed in their ways. Here is what a sample order looks like:

Sample Order

Each order is called a purchase order, or PO. On each order, you will see the ordering store's information and an itemized list of what the store is purchasing. You will also notice there is a box called 'Terms'. There, you will see how the store in question plans to pay for the order. They will either pay as soon as you ship the order, or within some period of time from then, usually 30 days after, which is called net 30 or n/30. Stores can either pay by credit card or check. If they are paying by credit card, then the credit card information may appear on the PO itself, or it may say that you have to call the store for it. Be prepared that calling the stores for a credit card is often an unpleasant situation because the person with the credit card is almost never there. You usually have to call multiple times and you may be made to feel uncomfortable. If you are not able to get the credit card information within a few tries, feel free to recruit your rep to help you.

When you are first starting out, you will be happy to give stores favorable payment terms like net 30, which is common. But you should know that there are a lot of stores that take advantage of favorable payment terms and do not pay for months or ever. Consequently, many jewelry designers have stopped giving favorable terms in general, or limit the availability of these payment terms to customers that they know purchase and pay regularly. It is perfectly acceptable to say that you will grant favorable payment terms, but only to customers who have already placed and paid for three orders with you in the past. I would recommend doing so unless a rep can vouch for the account.

Account Management

Processing and Shipping Orders

When you receive an order, you or your employees need to process it. You have to process future checks, charge the credit card upon shipment, or wait to do this, if you have extended payment terms, and then gather your materials to ship. For credit card orders, it is easy to find a merchant that will help you process these. Remember Merchant Warehouse I mentioned earlier?

Each order should include an invoice/packing list that contains an inventory of each piece included, along with prices of course. The invoice should also include whether or not the store has paid for its order and, if not, when payment is due. As a finishing touch, invoice should also include your contact information.

Stores expect to receive their merchandise as individually-wrapped and labeled jewelry pieces in individual small plastic bags, one piece of jewelry per bag. In the case of earrings, some stores will request to have them shipped on earring cards, but I would not include these unless you get a specific request. You can definitely charge stores for shipping. I usually charge $5 per shipment and $10 for unusually large shipments or if the store insists on shipping via UPS or FedEx. If you want to order insurance on your shipments, that cost usually falls on you - stores will not agree to pay for this.

You will need to develop a tracking system for orders, either online or in your own electronic records. This system will need to track all of your customers, what they have ordered, all of the pieces that you have shipped, the price per piece, what has been paid for, and which payments are due and when. You absolutely need to have an organized system up and running when you start filling orders and cannot leave these things for yourself or your employees to remember.

If you do not have a good tracking system, two things can happen: 1) you will have no way of knowing which stores did not pay you, and 2) you might track down stores that have already paid you, thinking that you are still owed money, and this can be very damaging to customer relationships.

You will also want to set up a calendaring service, such as Outlook or Google Alerts, to track when payments are due and also when the payments are 1 or 2 weeks overdue. For stores that are paying by credit card with favorable payment terms, and whose credit card information you have, it is your obligation to mark the date their payment is due and charge their credit card at the appropriate time. You may not charge your customers' credit cards even one day before the pre-agreed payment date, because stores plan their billing cycles carefully around these payment terms.

For customers whose credit card information you do not have, or who are expected to pay by check and are late in paying, you want to make sure that either you or your employees follow up with stores promptly on these pre-calendared dates. If you do not calendar due dates for payments and just have your orders sitting around in files, you will find that you are not be able to keep up with unpaid orders. You will be attempting to collect on them way past their due dates, which is always more difficult and hurts your business. Organization for payments is key.

In my business, I use a free file sharing service called 4shared.com to organize my orders. There are many others that can be found on the web. My employees maintain a separate folder for each store and in each folder they have paid and unpaid subfolders. When they first create an invoice, they save it in the unpaid folder. As soon I process payment, I move it to the paid folder. I do not allow myself to process any payments until I move the invoice into the paid folder first to avoid confusion.

In addition to the relationship with your customers, you need to make sure that you cut your reps their commission checks on a timely basis as well. That is another reason why the online management system is so important. My recommendation is to cut a check to your reps on each and every order that you process, right away. After I move the invoice to the correct folder, I then cut a commission check to my rep, and then process payment. I do these 3 things consecutively and do not even leave the desk between doing them, or else they are easy to forget. This order processing needs to become automated and second nature or mistakes are likely to be made.

Most reps are used to being paid their commissions on a monthly basis, but I find that with free bill-pay services there is no reason not to take care of this transaction immediately when processing orders. To have to do monthly reconciliations of all of your accounts is time consuming, and can lead to errors. I therefore recommend training yourself to do things in the above-mentioned order. One more thing about folders: you want to make sure to create new ones for each new year and not to mix years. This will make it much easier to work out your revenues or give the right information to your accountant when tax time comes around.

Another important set of items you will want to make sure to manage via your organized folder system is backorders, when stores order items that you do not currently have in stock. When this happens, you include this information in their invoice and packing list, write "quantity: 0" next to the item that was not in stock, do not charge them for it until you have the item to ship, and then you put the backordered items directly into your backorders folder for immediate follow-up. When an item is out of stock, it can sometimes be weeks before it is back and can be shipped out. If you do not have a good system of cataloging these items, you could very easily forget to ship it out and collect payment, and that is money lost from your business due to avoidable disorganization.

Client Relations

In general, your interests will be well-served by maintaining good, even friendly, relationships with clients. Going into stores personally to meet with owners and sales staff and to chat with them can pay great dividends. I do not do this myself as much anymore, but I certainly saw the benefits when I did. Clients tend to order more from designers that they enjoy a good relationship with. In addition, it is harder for clients to withhold payment or become difficult in other ways with designers they know personally. Therefore, you should be prepared, especially when you are starting out, to invest some time in developing personal client relations.

In order to maintain good relations and ensure that clients are always happy with you, be prepared to take back and swap out items that have not sold in stores. You should also be prepared to modify your designs to accommodate good clients' specific needs. It goes without saying that you should do everything you can to make sure that your process all orders and questions efficiently and that all of your merchandise is delivered on time.

Many stores and designers in the jewelry industry can be flaky and fail to do things that they promise, shipping things, sending payments, following up, etc. You want to make sure that you are not one of these people, that is, if you want to be in business for the long haul. You will notice that the stores that you have good relationships with will end up being reliable customers who pay on time and they will be reordering from you because you are a reliable supplier. A solid reputation is difficult to build but easy to destroy, so go above and beyond in terms of customer service.

Secrets of a Successful Jewelry Brand

Chapter 12

Selling Discontinued and Overstock Items

Selling Discontinued and Overstock Items

Discontinued and overstock items might seem at first like an after-thought in comparison to general sales, but it is actually a critical business issue. As your business grows and you introduce new designs, you will have items from old lines that remain unsold and pieces that you choose not to include in a new collection. There are always styles that do less well than others and as new styles come others must go.

When a style is selling well, you will likely have a lot of that style manufactured. Invariably, at some point in time that particular one will stop selling as well as before and you will be left with whatever's left on your hands. You will also have samples that come back from your reps and returned items that customers ship back to you after you think they have already sold. It is incredibly important to figure out how to sell those pieces to increase your cash flow and make sure you are not sitting with a ton of unused inventory on your hands that did not result in sales. That could be wasted money straight out of your pocket. Here are a few ideas, ranging from low tech to more sophisticated, that you can combine for maximum sales.

Craft Fairs and Farmers Markets

One way to get rid of discontinued items is to take them to craft fairs and farmers markets. I used this as my primary method of selling discontinued items for many years. Fairs and markets are extremely good for getting rid of discontinued items because each piece is sold individually and you can mark the discontinued pieces down to whatever price you want. You can also use these venues to test new products. I no longer go to fairs and markets, because my business is automated such that I no longer invest my own time working on sales. However, because I did this for years and know how lucrative fairs and markets can be, I felt obligated to mention them here. The money can be intoxicating. You can do this on a regular basis, or participate in just a couple of big fairs a year. While nobody will ever sell your product as well as you, you can consider getting someone else to sell for you at the markets, provided that you have a good inventory management system.

Sample Sales

You can also sell discontinued items at sample sales. Two examples of sample sales are Billion Dollar Babes and young designer markets. There are also miscellaneous shopping events hosted by organizations such as JenArt, Shecky's, and Lucky Magazine.

Consignment Stores

Another way to sell discontinued items is to get your items into consignment stores. I like to have my line in a couple of consignment stores at any given time in order to give them discontinued items.

Give-Aways!

Some of your good accounts will also ask or expect that you provide them with merchandise to give away at holiday parties, promotional events, and other functions. You should do this for the clients that generate a lot of sales for you, and this is a perfect way to use up discontinued or overstock pieces. Give-aways are also one of the best strategies for growing your social media fan base and keeping them engaged. Fans love getting free jewelry and amazing deals. This is what all the designers do. Trust me, you'll have plenty of things to give away. You will be asked on a regular basis to donate jewelry for events/auctions for every type of charity under the sun. You can use these as tax write offs and you can also talk about your contributions in your social media. Fans love that, too.

Off-Price Retailers

Off-price retailers such as TJ Maxx, Find Outlet, and others are also good options when it comes to selling discontinued or overstock merchandise. You should be aware though that these off-price retailers will often want to buy your merchandise at or below cost. They do, however, buy a lot and it is better to sell cheap than sit on the merchandise indefinitely without making back any of your money. Nickels vs Dimes.

Deal Websites

There are also websites that specialize in giving consumers incredible deals and sell high-end items for huge discounts. Examples of these are www.gilt.com, www.overstock.com, www.groupon.com, and www.zulilly.com. You can also sell lots of bulk items on Ebay.

Jewelry Parties and Trunk Shows

Another thing I no longer do, but which can be a great option for getting rid of discontinued merchandise, are privately-hosted jewelry parties sometimes called trunk shows. These parties are usually hosted by an individual at their house and invitations are usually spread by word of mouth. The host or hostess usually takes a commission and you are left with the rest. I am sure you are familiar with the jewelry party and trunk show model, as you may have started your business through this venue. As you grow your business and get into stores, you can think of jewelry parties and trunk shows as a great way to get rid of overstock merchandise, as opposed to being where your primary clientele comes from.

Selling Discontinued and Overstock Items

Your Own Online Shops

My favorite way to sell discontinued items is through my own shops on Etsy and Amazon. There are many other websites that allow you to create your own space, but Etsy and Amazon are by far the largest. These websites are convenient because, as mentioned above, they are not selective in terms of applicants like specific online stores that only carry a few brands, you can create your own space, include your brand's story, and upload all of the merchandise you will be offering for sale. I originally started selling online at these shops for the purpose of selling discontinued items, but this ended up being such a lucrative strategy that I am shifting more and more of my business to online sales, which will be the topic of my next book.

Thank you so much for joining me in this guide to taking your home jewelry business to the next level! I hope you have learned many new strategies and approaches, plus ideas and inspiration to grow your business. For years, I've been accumulating the thoughts for this book and I've always known that one day I would share them with the world. I've finally been able to do it with the help of my sister! I couldn't have done with without her.

I invite you to share your trials, tribulations, and successes on my blog www.YourOwnJewelryLine.com/blog and you can also email me at info@YourOwnJewelryLine.com . I would like to continue to help you as I find out what issues you're running into and what information is interesting to you.

If you find any information in this book to be no longer accurate, please email me at info@YourOwnJewelryLine.com so I can update it with the latest and greatest for everyone! I will continue to release free updates, so please email me if you'd like to receive those. Please check the blog for more content and use it as a forum to interact with me and each other.

And lastly, an honest and preferably kind review of this book would be incredibly helpful to other budding designers out there, as well as for me.

Thanks so much and see you on the blog!

About the Author

Efy Tal

I am the creator and designer of Efy Tal Jewelry www.EfyTal.com. I live and work in Glen Rock, New Jersey with my husband Ziggy and my little daughter Lia. I am most happy and proud to have created and life and a business where I can spend the day raising Lia at home while my business is running seamlessly in the background. To see more of the behind the scenes of my business, please LIKE my facebook page www.facebook.com/EfyTalJewelry

I am starting my new venture helping other moms and enterprising creative folks do what I have done through my new website www.YourOwnJewelryLine.com and my new facebook group www.facebook.com/YourOwnJewelryLine I hope you join me there!

Made in the USA
Monee, IL
26 January 2025